W9-BLY-541

**A
BOOK
OF
BOOK
LISTS**

A
BOOK
OF
BOOK
LISTS

Alex Johnson

For
Philip and Phyllis,
Wilma,
Thomas, Edward and Robert

First published 2017 by
The British Library
96 Euston Road
London NW1 2DB

Cataloguing in Publication Data
A catalogue record for this publication is available
from The British Library

ISBN 978 0 7123 5225 3

Typeset by Briony Hartley, Goldust Design
Cover by Rawshock Design
Printed and bound in Malta by Gutenberg Press

CONTENTS

Introduction   9

1. READING LISTS

Bin Laden's Bookshelf   11
Charles Darwin's 'to read' list   14
David Bowie's 100 influencers   17
Oscar Wilde's Reading Gaol bookcase   22
Every book Art Garfunkel has read since 1968   24
A prime minister's bookshelf   29
All the Presidents' books   32
Brian Eno's suggestions for the *Manual for Civilization*   36
Lubbock's 100 best books   39
Soldiers' reading lists: The solace of literature in
   the trenches   44
University reading lists   47
Premier League footballers' favourite reads   50
Dylan Thomas on Robert Browning   53
J.P. Morgan's annual summer reading list   53

2. ON THE MOVE

BookCrossing's most registered   57
Books left behind in hotels   60
Scott's *Discovery* library   63
Desert Island Discs: The books   67
Napoleon's travelling library   69

NeRD: The United States Navy's e-reader 71

3. IN THE LIBRARY

US Light House Establishment library box 141 75
A human library 78
David Byrne's private library: B 80
The Library of Babel 82
The books on the International Space Station 84
Lydia Languish's circulating library selection 89
A telephone box library 91
Mass Observation (1): Luccombe's typical bookcases 94
MPs' most-borrowed books 96
Queen Mary's doll's house library 99
Scottish prisoners' favourite books 101
Marilyn Monroe's private library 103

4. JUNIOR CHOICE

The books Alan Turing borrowed from his school library 105
Mass Observation (2): Books borrowed by children
  visiting libraries in Fulham in May 1940 108
Thom Gunn's poetry recommendations for children 113

5. UNWANTED

Burnt by the Nazis 117
Most-challenged books in America 119
The most-unread books 121
Joe Orton's damaged books 123
Most popular out-of-print books 126
Banned books at Guantánamo Detainee Library 129

6. ON THE SCREEN

Big Bang Theory: The art of the television bookshelf 133
The *Dead Poets Society* poems 136
The Wrath of Khan: A *Star Trek* bookshelf 138
A *Good Will Hunting* historiography 141
Murph's *Interstellar* bookshelf 143

7. LISTS YET TO COME

Future classics 147
Future library 149

8. ADVENTURES IN BOOKS

Everything in Shavian 153
Books annotated by David Foster Wallace 155
Bjargvætturinn í grasinu: *The Catcher in the Rye* in translation 158
Books 'written' by Sherlock Holmes 160
Winners of the Bookseller/Diagram Prize 164
Books that have never been written 167
The fake books of Charles Dickens 170
Kansas City Library's Community Bookshelf 175
Lost books 178
Not *The Great Gatsby* 180
The first audiobooks (and other sensory fiction) 183
The UK's top twenty revisited reads 187
Books owned by Richard III 190
Bibliotherapy: Books on Prescription 192
Book list art 195
Books IKEA uses as decoration in its shops 197
Bibliomemoirs: A list of book-list books 200

INTRODUCTION

To tell people what to read is, as a rule, either useless or harmful;
for the appreciation of literature is a question of temperament
not of teaching.
Oscar Wilde

This is a book of book lists. Not of the '1,001 Books You MUST Read Before You're 40' variety (although there is a section on the men who started this trend), but lists that tell stories. These are unique collections of titles. Some are not real, but all are revealing. As novelist Walter Mosley has pointed out, a person's bookcase tells you everything you need to know about them.

Sadly, many of the books mentioned are no longer in print. Happily, second-hand bookshops still stock the majority of these titles, while Project Gutenberg and the Internet Archive often provide free online alternatives.

Chapter One
READING LISTS

BIN LADEN'S BOOKSHELF

Handbook of International Law by Anthony Aust

Civil Democratic Islam: Partners, Resources, and Strategies by Cheryl Benard

Killing Hope: U.S. Military and CIA Interventions since World War II by William Blum

Rogue State: A Guide to the World's Only Superpower by William Blum

Necessary Illusions: Thought Control in Democratic Societies by Noam Chomsky

Fortifying Pakistan: The Role of U.S. Internal Security Assistance (only the book's introduction) by Christine Fair and Peter Chalk

Hegemony or Survival: America's Quest for Global Dominance by Noam Chomsky

America's 'War on Terrorism' by Michel Chossudovsky

Conspirators' Hierarchy: The Committee of 300 by John Coleman

New Political Religions, or Analysis of Modern Terrorism by Barry Cooper

Guerilla Air Defense: Antiaircraft Weapons and Techniques

for *Guerilla Forces* by James Crabtree
New Pearl Harbor: Disturbing Questions about the Bush Administration and 9/11 by David Ray Griffin
Christianity and Islam in Spain 756–1031 A.D. by C.R. Haines
The Secret Teachings of All Ages by Manly Hall
Black Box Voting, Ballot Tampering in the 21st Century by Bev Harris
The U.S. and Vietnam 1787–1941 by Robert Hopkins Miller
Military Intelligence Blunders by John Hughes-Wilson
A Brief Guide to Understanding Islam by I.A. Ibrahim
International Relations Theory and the Asia-Pacific by John Ikenberry and Michael Mastandano
The Rise and Fall of the Great Powers by Paul Kennedy
In Pursuit of Allah's Pleasure by Asim Abdul Maajid, Esaam-ud-Deen and Dr Naahah Ibrahim
The 2030 Spike by Colin Mason
America's Strategic Blunders by Willard Matthias
Secrets of the Federal Reserve by Eustace Mullins
Unfinished Business, U.S. Overseas Military Presence in the 21st Century by Michael O'Hanlon
Confessions of an Economic Hit Man by John Perkins
The Best Democracy Money Can Buy by Greg Palast
Bounding the Global War on Terror by Jeffrey Record
Al-Qaeda's Online Media Strategies: From Abu Reuter to Irhabi 007 by Hanna Rogan
Crossing the Rubicon by Michael Ruppert
Imperial Hubris by Michael Scheuer
Checking Iran's Nuclear Ambitions by Henry Sokolski and Patrick Clawson
The Taking of America 1-2-3 by Richard Sprague
Bloodlines of the Illuminati by Fritz Springmeier

The Best Enemy Money Can Buy by Anthony Sutton
Oxford History of Modern War by Charles Townsend
Obama's Wars by Bob Woodward
Project MKULTRA, the CIA's program of research in behavioral modification. Joint hearing before the Select Committee on Intelligence and the Subcommittee on Health and Scientific Research of the Committee on Human Resources, United States Senate, Ninety-fifth Congress, first session, August 3, 1977. United States. Congress. Senate. Select Committee on Intelligence

Not only did the US Navy SEALs who raided the Abbottabad compound in Pakistan in 2011 find Osama bin Laden, they also discovered his collection of books. These reading materials are being analysed and gradually made public by the US government under the title of 'Bin Laden's Bookshelf' and the above is a list of the English-language books found at his home, all digital copies rather than printed.

There is no light reading here. Instead of laughing at Bertie Wooster's controversial choice of purple socks, the head of al-Qaida seems to have preferred high-profile critics of the US government such as Chomsky and Palast, while concentrating entirely on serious politics, law and, especially, conspiracy theories. Among these are the chronicles of the ongoing activities of the Illuminati, the running of the USA by shadowy cabals (take your pick of a Power Control Group, elite financiers or 300 chosen families), and that 9/11 was organised or at the very least allowed to happen by the US government. Interestingly, Michael Scheuer, who wrote *Imperial Hubris* (included in this list), once ran the CIA's Bin Laden tracking unit.

The full collection also contains dozens of reports and think tank publications on al-Qaida and similar groups, such as *The 9/11 Commission Report*, the official account of the terrorist attacks.

The US authorities have not given any precise details about where the books were found in the residence or what was on his 'to read' pile on his bedside table. A second list features titles which may have been read by Bin Laden, but according to the US government were probably used by other people living in the compound.

This is a more eclectic selection and includes *Grappler's Guide to Sports Nutrition* by John Berardi and Michael Fry, the 2008 *Guinness Book of World Records* (Children's Edition), *Is It the Heart Which You Are Asking?* (a suicide prevention guide), and a guide to the Delta Force Extreme 2 first-person shooter video game. There were also a couple of Arabic–English dictionaries and the December 2010 *Popular Science* magazine's 'Best Innovations of the Year' Issue.

CHARLES DARWIN'S 'TO READ' LIST

Humboldt's *New Spain*
Richardson's *Fauna Borealis*
Entomological Magazine
Decandolle Philosophic on Geographical distrib in Dict.
   Sciences Nat.in Geolog Soc.
F Cuvier on instinct
L Jenyns paper in *Annals of Nat. History*
Roy St.Vincent vol. iii p. 164 on unfixed form
Dr Royle on Himalaya types

Smellie *Philosophy of Zoology*
Falconer remark on the influence of climate
White regular gradation in Man
Lindley introduction to the Natural System
Bevan on honey bee
Dutrochet memoires sur les vegetaux et animaux – on sleep
   & movements of Plants £1. 4s
Prichard; a 3d vol.
Voyage aux terres Australes chapt. xxxix, tom iv. p. 273
Latreille *Geographie des insectes* 8° p. 181

Starting in 1838 and continuing on and off until 1860, Charles Darwin jotted down in his notebooks the books he planned to read (he then sometimes went back and crossed out those he had finished). The notes were quite detailed, so that as well as the title and author, he sometimes also included libraries or people who might be able to lend him a copy.

Darwin's son Francis says his father had a very methodical way of approaching his reading. 'He had one shelf on which were piled up the books he had not yet read, and another to which they were transferred after having been read, and before being catalogued. He would often groan over his unread books, because there were so many which he knew he should never read.'

The list above is a verbatim selection of some of the early entries, among them James Cowles Prichard's 1813 five-volume *Researches into the physical history of Man*, a key anthropological text about evolution and natural selection. Other major titles include Thomas Malthus on *Population* and Adam Smith's *Theory of Moral Sentiments*, but it was an eclectic mix which also featured Alexandre Jean Baptiste

Parent-Duchâlet's 1836 *De la prostitution dans la ville de Paris considéré sous le rapport de l'hygiène publique, de la morale et de l'administration* as well as Daniel Defoe's *Robinson Crusoe*. Other books include various works by William Shakespeare (*Hamlet, Othello, A Midsummer Night's Dream*), Jane Austen's *Mansfield Park*, biographies of Wesley and Cicero, and Virgil's *Georgics*.

As it was a personal list, not intended for publication, the notebooks also contain various comments:

> Read Aristotle to see whether any of my views are ancient
> Haller's Physiology — My Father thinks would contain facts for me
> Pliny's Nat. Hist of world {Well skimmed}
> Failed in reading Niebuhr's Rome
> Swift. Stella's Journal amusing

Not all of these comments were entirely positive. On 15 March 1839, Darwin notes: 'Skimmed Pope & Dryden's Poems — need not try them again' and on 7 May the following year, having looked into Abraham Tucker's seven-volume 'The light of nature pursued', felt moved to add: 'Skimmed a little of Tucker's light of nature. Intolerably prolix.'

'When I see the list of books of all kinds which I read and abstracted, including whole series of Journals and Transactions, I am surprised at my industry,' Darwin wrote in his autobiography. Personal and work libraries certainly played a central part in his life. On board the HMS *Beagle* was a library of around 400 volumes, housed in Darwin's own cabin. Painstaking research has reconstructed much of it and turned it into a searchable online resource at darwin-online.org.uk where you can search alphabetically or by category.

Among the titles are Milton's *Paradise Lost*, the *Encyclopaedia Britannica* (6th edition, twenty volumes, plus a one-volume supplement), James Cook's account of exploring the Pacific Ocean and Sharon Turner's 1832 'The sacred history of the world, as displayed in the Creation and subsequent events to the Deluge, attempted to be philosophically considered in a series of letters to a son (2nd edition)'.

By category, it can be broken down as:

Travel/Voyages 36%
Natural history 33%
Geology 15%
Atlases/Nautical 7%
Literature 4%
Reference 3%
History 2%

As well as 125 English titles, there were thirty-eight in French, nine in Spanish, seven in German, one in Latin and one in Greek.

DAVID BOWIE'S 100 INFLUENCERS

Hawksmoor by Peter Ackroyd
Inferno by Dante Alighieri
Money by Martin Amis
The Fire Next Time by James Baldwin
Flaubert's Parrot by Julian Barnes
Herzog by Saul Bellow
Room at the Top by John Braine

Kafka was the Rage by Anatole Broyard
The Master and Margarita by Mikhail Bulgakov
Zanoni by Edward Bulwer-Lytton
Earthly Powers by Anthony Burgess
A Clockwork Orange by Anthony Burgess
Silence: Lectures and Writing by John Cage
The Stranger by Albert Camus
In Cold Blood by Truman Capote
Nights at the Circus by Angela Carter
Wonder Boys by Michael Chabon
The Songlines by Bruce Chatwin
Awopbopaloobop Alopbambboom: The Golden Age of Rock
    by Nik Cohn
David Bomberg by Richard Cork
Writers At Work: The Paris Review Interviews edited by
    Malcolm Cowley
The Bridge by Hart Crane
Beyond the Brillo Box by Arthur C. Danto
White Noise by Don DeLillo
The Brief Wondrous Life of Oscar Wao by Junot Díaz
Berlin Alexanderplatz by Alfred Döblin
Strange People by Frank Edwards
The Waste Land by T.S. Eliot
As I Lay Dying by William Faulkner
A People's Tragedy by Orlando Figes
The Great Gatsby by F. Scott Fitzgerald
Madame Bovary by Gustave Flaubert
Before the Deluge by Otto Friedrich
The Sound of the City: The Rise of Rock And Roll by Charlie Gillett
Journey into the Whirlwind by Eugenia Ginzburg
Sweet Soul Music: Rhythm and Blues and the Southern Dream

of Freedom by Peter Guralnick

Hall's Dictionary of Subjects and Symbols in Art by James A. Hall

On Having No Head by Douglass Harding

Nowhere to Run: The Story of Soul Music by Gerri Hirshey

The Trial of Henry Kissinger by Christopher Hitchens

The Iliad by Homer

Mr Norris Changes Trains by Christopher Isherwood

The Age of American Unreason by Susan Jacoby

The Origin of Consciousness in the Breakdown of the Bicameral Mind by Julian Jaynes

On the Road by Jack Kerouac

All the Emperor's Horses by David Kidd

Darkness at Noon by Arthur Koestler

The Divided Self by R.D. Laing

The Leopard by Giuseppe di Lampedusa

Passing by Nella Larson

Maldodor by Comte de Lautréamont

Lady Chatterley's Lover by D.H. Lawrence

Metropolitan Life by Fran Lebowitz

Transcendental Magic, its Doctrine and Ritual by Eliphas Lévi

Blast by Wyndham Lewis

Mystery Train by Greil Marcus

In Between the Sheets by Ian McEwan

Puckoon by Spike Milligan

The Sailor Who Fell from Grace with the Sea by Yukio Mishima

The American Way of Death by Jessica Mitford

Lolita by Vladimir Nabokov

The Bird Artist by Howard Norman

McTeague by Frank Norris

Selected Poems by Frank O'Hara

Inside the Whale and Other Essays by George Orwell

1984 by George Orwell

The Hidden Persuaders by Vance Packard

The Gnostic Gospels by Elaine Pagels

Sexual Personae: Art and Decadence from Nefertiti to Emily Dickinson by Camille Paglia

The 42nd Parallel by John Dos Passos

The Street by Ann Petry

A Grave for a Dolphin by Alberto Denti di Pirajno

English Journey by J.B. Priestley

City of Night by John Rechy

Octobriana and the Russian Underground by Peter Sadecky

Tales of Beatnik Glory by Ed Saunders

Teenage by Jon Savage

Last Exit to Brooklyn by Hubert Selby, Jr

In Bluebeard's Castle by George Steiner

Interviews with Francis Bacon by David Sylvester

The Prime of Miss Jean Brodie by Muriel Spark

The Coast of Utopia by Tom Stoppard

The Insult by Rupert Thomson

Infants of the Spring by Wallace Thurman

A Confederacy of Dunces by John Kennedy Toole

Billy Liar by Keith Waterhouse

Fingersmith by Sarah Waters

Vile Bodies by Evelyn Waugh

Mr Wilson's Cabinet of Wonders by Lawrence Weschler

The Day of the Locust by Nathanael West

The Outsider by Colin Wilson

The Quest for Christa T by Christa Wolf

The Life and Times of Little Richard by Charles White

Black Boy by Richard Wright

Tadanori Yokoo by Tadanori Yokoo

A People's History of the United States by Howard Zinn
Beano comic
Raw comic
Viz comic
Private Eye magazine

David Bowie was a keen reader who said he took several hundred books to Mexico for the shooting of the 1976 film *The Man Who Fell To Earth*, all stored in a kind of travelling library. 'I had these cabinets and they were rather like the boxes that amplifiers get packed up in,' he revealed. Co-star Buck Henry added that he noticed the limousine in which Bowie was driven around had a boot full of books.

Two years before his death, Bowie released a list of the 100 books that provided the most creative influence for the *David Bowie Is* exhibition about his life and work. It is a list of books he felt were important rather than his actual 100 favourite reads.

The original list also includes brief details of each of the books mentioned. For example, his copy of the *Iliad* is a late 1970s paperback, his *Mr Norris Changes Trains* by Christopher Isherwood is a 1960s Penguin rather than the 1935 first edition, and George Steiner's *In Bluebeard's Castle: Some Notes towards the Redefinition of Culture* is a hardback from the early 1970s.

OSCAR WILDE'S READING GAOL BOOKCASE

Collected Works of Matthew Arnold
City of God by St Augustine
The Confessions of St Augustine
Various Works by Charles Baudelaire
The Pilgrim's Progress by John Bunyan
The Prioress's Tale by Geoffrey Chaucer
The Divine Comedy by Dante Alighieri
La Vita Nuova by Dante Alighieri
Collected Works of John Dryden
Trois Contes by Gustave Flaubert
La Tentation de St Antoin by Gustave Flaubert
Illumination by Harold Frederic
The Passes of the Pyrenees by Charles L. Freeston
Faust by Johann Wolfgang von Goethe
Brittany by Baring Gould
Collected Works of Hafiz
The Well-Beloved by Thomas Hardy
The Longer Poems of John Keats
Epic and Romance: Essays on Medieval Literature by William
    Paton Ker
The Courtship of Morrice Buckler: A Romance by A.E.W. Mason
An Essay on Comedy by George Meredith
The History of the Jews by Henry Hart Milman
History of Latin Christianity by Henry Hart Milman
History of Rome by Theodor Mommsen
Juvenile Offenders by William Douglas Morrison
A History of Ancient Greek Literature by Gilbert Murray
Apologia Pro Vita Sua by John Henry Newman
Two Essays on Miracles by John Henry Newman

Idea of a University by John Henry Newman
Essays on Grace by John Henry Newman
Provincial Letters by Blaise Pascal
Pensées by Blaise Pascal
The Renaissance by Walter Pater
Gaston de Latour by Walter Pater
Miscellaneous Studies by Walter Pater
Egyptian Decorative Art (paperback) by W.M. Flinders Petrie
Letters and Memoir by Dante Gabriel Rossetti
Quo Vadis by Henryk Sienkiewicz
The Student's Chaucer by Walter William Skeat
Collected Works of Edmund Spenser
Treasure Island by Robert Lewis Stevenson
Collected Works of August Strindberg
The Study of Dante by J.A. Symons
Richard Wagner's letters to August Roeckel
Collected Works of William Wordsworth

In 1895 Oscar Wilde was sentenced to two years of hard labour for gross indecency and was shuttled between Newgate, Pentonville and Wandsworth prisons before finally reaching Reading. Initially, his access to books was extremely limited but eventually he was allowed to build up a small library, examples of which were put on display at HM Prison Reading in 2016 and are listed above.

During prisoners' first three months behind bars they were only allowed to read a prayer book, a hymn book and the Bible, but after special pleading by Liberal MP Richard Haldane, the authorities relented (Wilde gave the Governor at Reading a special signed copy of *The Importance Of Being Earnest* as a thank you present for allowing more books in). Wilde was not only allowed to keep books in his cell, he was also permitted to leave his light on as late as he wanted to read them.

The first titles he asked for in June 1895 were *The Confessions of St Augustine*, various volumes of works by Baudelaire and Cardinal Newman, and one of the key books in his life, *The Renaissance* by Walter Pater. This was a leading text in the aesthetic movement and instilled in Wilde the drive to turn his life into a work of art. 'The Library here contains no example of Thackeray's or Dickens's novels,' he wrote in one of his requests for new books. 'I feel sure that a complete set of their works would be as great a boon to many amongst the other prisoners as it certainly would be to myself.'

Wilde was declared bankrupt and his personal library at home was split up and auctioned. Only around fifty are available in public collections and around 3,000 have never been tracked down. A reconstructed version is available on the Library Thing site (www.librarything.com) and explored in huge detail in Thomas Wright's book *Built of Books: How Reading Defined the Life of Oscar Wilde*, which also reveals Wilde's tendency to tear off and eat the top corner of each page as he read it.

EVERY BOOK ART GARFUNKEL HAS READ SINCE 1968

The End of the Road by John Barth
The Art of Loving by Erich Fromm
Brave New World by Aldous Huxley

Johann Sebastian Bach, an Introduction to his Life and Works
   by Russell H. Miles
In Search of the Miraculous by P.D. Ouspensky
Boyhood with Gurdjieff by Fritz Peters
The Confessions by Jean-Jacques Rousseau
Romeo and Juliet by William Shakespeare
My Life and Hard Times by James Thurber
The Adventures of Huckleberry Finn by Mark Twain

Art Garfunkel is a particularly keen reader and on his website publishes a list of every book he has read since June 1968. Above is the very start of what he calls his 'Library', running from June to November 1968. In an interview with the *New Yorker* in 2008, he emphasises that: 'I avoid fluff ... The stuff that men are always reading on planes. I don't read that.'

   Below is January to March 1992:

The Art of Courtly Love by Andreas Capellanus
The Sound and the Fury by William Faulkner
An Outline of Psycho-Analysis by Sigmund Freud
The Vintage Mencken by H.L. Mencken
The Scarlet Pimpernel by Baroness Orczy
The Narrative of Arthur Gordon Pym by Edgar Allan Poe
The Sermon on the Mount according to Vendanta by Swami
   Prabhavananda
Dr Jekyll and Mr Hyde by Robert Louis Stevenson
A Short History of the World by H.G. Wells
The Truly Disadvantaged by William Julius Wilson

Screenwriter and film director Steven Soderbergh has also put together a couple of similar lists for 2009 and 2010 (both of which also included all the television shows and films he'd watched). Here is his book list for everything he read in 2009:

Animal Spirits; How Human Psychology Drives the Economy and Why it Matters for Global Capitalism by George A. Akerlof and Robert Shiller
Human Smoke by Nicholson Baker
Vox by Nicholson Baker
40 Stories by Donald Barthelme
3 Nights in August by Buzz Bissinger
Columbine by Dave Cullen
The Race Card by Richard Thompson Ford
The Failure by James Greer
Conversations with Robert Evans by Lawrence Grobel
Conversations with Marlon Brando by Lawrence Grobel
Pictures at a Revolution by Mark Harris
Digital Barbarism by Mark Helprin
Things I Didn't Know by Robert Hughes
The Ridiculous Race by Steve Hely and Vali Chandrasekaran
The Cult of the Amateur by Andrew Keen
Appetite for Self-Destruction by Steve Knopper
Where the Dead Lay by David Levien
Moneyball by Michael Lewis
Remainder by Tom McCarthy
Inherent Vice by Thomas Pynchon
Arsenals of Folly by Richard Rhodes
Musicophilia by Oliver Sacks
Straw: Finding My Way by Darryl Strawberry

This is Water by David Foster Wallace
Was Clara Schumann a Fag Hag? by David Watkin

When Cambridge University Press published Volume 2 of Samuel Beckett's letters, they highlighted what the great playwright was reading between 1941 and 1956. Although generally positive, Beckett felt moved to say that in his copy of *Mosquitoes* by William Faulkner, he was less pleased 'with a preface by Queneau that would make an ostrich puke'.

Lautreamont and Sade by Maurice Blanchot
The Stranger by Albert Camus
The Temptation to Exist by Emil Cioran
Journey to the End of the Night by Louis-Ferdinand Céline
Crooked House by Agatha Christie ('very tired Christie')
Effi Briest by Theodor Fontane
The Hunchback of Notre Dame by Victor Hugo
The Castle by Franz Kafka
Man's Fate by André Malraux
The 628-E8 by Octave Mirbeau
Repeat Performance by William O'Farrell ('Excellent, once past
  the beginning')
Andromaque by Jean Racine
The Catcher in the Rye by J.D. Salinger
Around the World in 80 Days by Jules Verne

One of the most consistent book-listers is Nick Hornby, whose lighthearted 'Stuff I've Been Reading' columns in *The Believer* magazine (consequently collected in various volumes not listed in this chapter) have catalogued his monthly Books Bought and Books Read reckonings since 2003. Here's what May 2011 looked like:

BOOKS BOUGHT:
A Visit from the Goon Squad by Jennifer Egan
Norwood by Charles Portis
Out Stealing Horses by Per Petterson
The Harvard Psychedelic Club: How Timothy Leary, Ram Dass, Huston Smith, and Andrew Weil Killed the Fifties and Ushered in a New Age for America by Don Lattin
Ball of Fire: The Tumultuous Life and Comic Art of Lucille Ball by Stefan Kanfer
Unincorporated Persons in the Late Honda Dynasty by Tony Hoagland

BOOKS READ:
Marry Me: A Romance by John Updike
The Psychopath Test: A Journey Through the Madness Industry by Jon Ronson
Friday Night Lights by H.G. Bissinger
My Name Is Mina by David Almond

'I bought so many books this month it's obscene,' he wrote for the July 2004 column, 'and I'm not owning up to them all: this is a selection. And to be honest, I've been economical with the truth for months now. I keep finding books that I bought, didn't read, and didn't list.'

A PRIME MINISTER'S BOOKSHELF

The Last Testament by Sam Bourne
Blood & Rage by Michael Burleigh
The Blair Years by Alastair Campbell
Alastair Cooke's America
Thinking the Unthinkable by Richard Cockett
Book of the Dead by Patricia Cornwell
The Glassbook of the Dreameaters by G.W. Dahlquist
Engleby by Sebastian Faulks
A Million Bullets by James Fergusson
The Outcast by Sadie Jones
Austerity Britain by David Kynaston
Dark Continent by Mark Mazower
Cloud Atlas by David Mitchell
Brown's Britain by Robert Peston
The Spin Doctor's Diary by Lance Price
August 1914 by Alexander Solzhenitsyn
Saturn's Children by Charles Stross
Douglas Hurd: The Public Servant by Mark Stuart
Judgment: How Winning Leaders Make Great Calls by Noel
    Tichy and Warren Bennis
Chambers Book of Speeches

Bookshelves are great for branding. If we are what we read, a bookshelf becomes a public mirror for anybody who wants to find out who we really are or who we want to suggest we are, something about us that perhaps isn't so easily seen. Sometimes books have nothing to do with reading.

When David Cameron was interviewed by Andrew Marr for the BBC in 2009 in the agonisingly long build-up to the 2010 General Election, the meeting took place in the MP's home in West London. This gave eagle-eyed viewers the chance to virtually browse the future Prime Minister's bookcase, conveniently situated behind his chair.

Apart from perhaps the Sam Bourne, there are few guilty pleasures here or indications of obsessional fandom. Nor are they arranged in any particular order, by spine colour, or alphabetically. It's heavy on worthy reads, recent history, politics and key issues such as terrorism, Afghanistan and spin doctoring, but also features a fairly eclectic range of fiction (thrillers, literary fiction and genre-bending – *Saturn's Children* is a science-fiction novel in which humans have become extinct and a female courtesan robot becomes involved in a class robot struggle …).

Although it is impossible to decipher every title on the bookshelf, it may also contain Mr Cameron's stated favourite books, Robert Graves's *Goodbye to All That* and Hugh Fearnley-Whittingstall's *The River Cottage Cookbook*, which he chose on *Desert Island Discs*. His favourite children's book, *Our Island Story* by Henrietta Elizabeth Marshall, is probably in one of his children's bedrooms.

The Camerons' bookshelves continued to dominate the post-election news agenda, appearing in their Downing Street flat when German Chancellor Angela Merkel visited the Prime Minister and Michelle Obama visited his wife Samantha. Again, there was close scrutiny of the titles in their kitchen/dining area (as well as the bookshelf itself, £665 from Oka) which included:

Mrs Beeton's Book of Household Management
The Essential House Book by Terence Conran

Art and Artists by Jeremy Kingston
Provence Interiors and Paris Interiors by Lisa Lovatt-Smith
On Royalty by Jeremy Paxman
The Flavour Thesaurus by Niki Segnit
Complete Works of William Shakespeare
The River Cottage Every Day by Hugh Fearnley-Whittingstall
The Ginger Pig Meat Book by Tim Wilson and Fran Warde
The Abs Diet by David Zinczenko and Ted Spiker

Although press comments about the intellectual nature of their content were not wholly positive, this seems slightly harsh as few of us keep our Proust in the pantry.

Social media has added a whole new dimension to the game of political book-spotting, as Scottish Conservative leader Ruth Davidson discovered when she tweeted a photo of herself at home watching television (specifically Andy Murray playing at Wimbledon).

Among the books that could be seen on the bookshelves behind her were:

Economics for Dummies by Peter Antonioni and Sean Masaki
   Flynn
World Politics by Peter Calvocoressi
*The Right Word at the Right Time: A Guide to the English
   Language and How to Use It* by John Ellison Kahn
Power Trip: A Decade of Policy, Plots and Spin by Damian McBride
Daniel Defoe: Master of Fictions by Maximillian E. Novak
The Downing Street Years by Margaret Thatcher
The Bible
Oxford Dictionary of Economics

In the 2015 UK General Election campaign, UKIP's then deputy leader Paul Nuttall appeared in a promotional photograph standing in front of a bookshelf full of books. However, some of these appear to have been photoshopped in and at least one pile of books can be seen twice in the image. Replying to this charge, Mr Nuttall tweeted: 'It's not true. I just have two copies of every book!'

ALL THE PRESIDENTS' BOOKS

Barbarian Days: A Surfing Life by William Finnegan
The Girl on the Train by Paula Hawkins
H Is for Hawk by Helen Macdonald
Seveneves by Neal Stephenson
The Underground Railroad by Colson Whitehead

One of the annual traditions of Barack Obama's presidency was the announcement of his annual summer holiday reading list. Above is his final list in 2016, and below is what he chose the year before:

Washington: A Life by Ron Chernow
Between the World and Me by Ta-Nehisi Coates
All The Light We Cannot See by Anthony Doerr
The Sixth Extinction by Elizabeth Kolbert
The Lowland by Jhumpa Lahiri

But he is only the latest in a long line of Presidents who enjoyed reading, starting with Thomas Jefferson, who owned so many books in his private library that he was able to donate most of it to the government to replace the Library of Congress, which was burnt by British soldiers in 1812. His various letters to friends with suggested reading lists are frighteningly long and erudite. Jefferson's successor, John Adams (Obama included David McCullough's biography of him in his 2009 list), was also well read and had a habit of annotating his books heavily, adding an extra 10,000 words to *An Historical and Moral View of the Origin and Progress of the French Revolution* by Mary Wollstonecraft.

More recently, John F. Kennedy's list of favourite books reflected his interest in the work of Ian Fleming – and James Bond – and sales of *From Russia With Love* were greatly helped by his public endorsement of it. These are the other titles:

The Price of Union by Herbert Agar
John Quincy Adams by Samuel Flagg Bemis
Montrose by John Buchan
Pilgrim's Way by John Buchan
Lord Melbourne by David Cecil
Marlborough by Sir Winston Churchill
John C. Calhoun by Margaret L. Coit
Talleyrand by Duff Cooper
The Emergence of Lincoln by Allan Nevins
Byron in Italy by Peter Quennell
The Red and the Black by M. de Stendhal

Apparently Hillary Clinton remarked on the need to build more bookshelves into the White House when she and her husband Bill first moved in. Bill's list of his twenty-one favourite books includes Marcus Aurelius's *Meditations*, which he apparently re-reads every couple of years, as well as his wife's memoir:

I Know Why the Caged Bird Sings by Maya Angelou

Meditations by Marcus Aurelius

The Denial of Death by Ernest Becker

Parting the Waters: America in the King Years 1954–1963 by
   Taylor Branch

Living History by Hillary Rodham Clinton

Lincoln by David Herbert Donald

The Four Quartets by T.S. Eliot

Invisible Man by Ralph Ellison

*The Way of the World: From the Dawn of Civilizations to the
   Eve of the Twenty-First Century* by David Fromkin

One Hundred Years of Solitude by Gabriel García Márquez

The Cure at Troy: A Version of Sophocles' Philoctetes by Seamus
   Heaney

*King Leopold's Ghost: A Story of Greed, Terror and Heroism in
   Colonial Africa* by Adam Hochschild

The Imitation of Christ by Thomas à Kempis

Homage to Catalonia by George Orwell

*The Evolution of Civilizations: An Introduction to Historical
   Analysis* by Carroll Quigley

Moral Man and Immoral Society: A Study in Ethics and Politics
   by Reinhold Niebuhr

The Confessions of Nat Turner by William Styron

Politics as a Vocation by Max Weber

You Can't Go Home Again by Thomas Wolfe

Nonzero: The Logic of Human Destiny by Robert Wright

The Collected Poems of W.B. Yeats

Sandwiched between Clinton and Obama was President George W. Bush. Despite Bush's reputation in the media for not being a book-lover, his former senior adviser and deputy chief of staff Karl Rove revealed that the two of them had an annual competition to see who could read the most books in a year. According to Rove, as well as reading the Bible every twelve months, the President also enjoyed a wide range of fiction and non-fiction, from Albert Camus's *L'Étranger* and Hugh Thomas's *The Spanish Civil War* to numerous Travis McGee mysteries by John MacDonald.

Some Presidents also write books. According to Donald Trump's website, 'All of Mr. Trump's personally written books have been bestsellers. For once, the mind of this internationally renowned business mogul is an open book.' This is that list:

Crippled America
Time to Get Tough
The Art of the Deal
The Art of the Comeback
The America We Deserve
The Trump Card: Playing to Win in Work and Life by Ivanka
    Trump
The Way to the Top
How to Get Rich
Think Like a Billionaire
The Best Golf Advice I Ever Received
Why We Want You To Be Rich
The Best Real Estate Advice I Ever Received
Think Big and Kick Ass
Never Give Up

Think Like a Champion
Midas Touch

BRIAN ENO'S SUGGESTIONS FOR
THE MANUAL FOR CIVILIZATION

A *Pattern Language* by Christopher Alexander et al.
The *Illustrated Flora of Britain and Northern Europe* by Marjorie
    Blamey and Christopher Grey Wilson
The Discoverers by Daniel Boorstin
The Wheels of Commerce by Fernand Braudel
Crowds and Power by Elias Canetti
Printing and the Mind of Man by John Carter and Percy Muir
Dancing in the Streets by Barbara Ehrenreich
Roll Jordan Roll by Eugene Genovese
Mother Nature: A History of Mothers, Infants, and Natural
    Selection by Sarah Hardy
The Face of Battle by John Keegan
The Cambridge World History of Food (two volumes) by
    Kenneth F. Kiple and Kriemhild Coneè Ornelas
The Mind in the Cave: Consciousness and the Origins of Art by
    David Lewis-Williams
A History of the World in 100 Objects by Neil MacGregor
Peter the Great: His Life and World by Richard Massie
Keeping Together in Time by William McNeill
Contingency, Irony and Solidarity by Richard Rorty
The Confidence Trap by David Runciman
Seeing Like a State by James C. Scott
War and Peace by Leo Tolstoy
The Notebooks by Leonardo da Vinci

What happens when a [insert your catastrophe of choice here] happens? While many people will be most worried about clean water, shelter and the location of their loved ones, there will also be those grieving over the mass destruction of our libraries and bookshops. But fear not! The farsighted people at San Francisco's the Long Now Foundation have put together a kind of *Desert Island Discs* 'must read' list of around 3,500 books – they call it the *Manual for Civilization* – which they feel will best keep us going through the disaster and help us rebuild everything a bit. In the meantime, it is available in conventional library format at their public space, The Interval.

The books selected fall into four categories and cover far more than basic survival techniques:

Cultural Canon (iconic authors such as Shakespeare and Plato)
Mechanics of Civilization (technical knowledge, how to build and understand how things work)
Rigorous Science Fiction (books that tell potentially useful stories about a hypothetical future)
Long-term Thinking, Futurism, and relevant history (works which focus on how to think about the future, some including surveys of the past)

The list is largely put together by Long Now staff and members, but famous creatives with particular areas of interest have also been invited to submit short lists of ideas. The one above contains all musician Brian Eno's suggestions under the heading of 'long-term thinking' and other contributors include Violet Blue (human sexuality), Ami Burnham (reproduction and birth) and astronomer Jill

Tartar (first contact). Here is sci-fi writer Neal Stevenson's selection of useful history books:

The American Practical Navigator: An Epitome of Navigation by Nathaniel Bowditch
Civilization & Capitalism 15th–18th Century, Volumes 1–3, by Fernand Braudel
Newton's Principia for the Common Reader by S. Chandrasekhar
Marlborough, His Life & Times, Volumes 1–6, by Winston Churchill
Son of The Morning Star: Custer and the Little Bighorn by Evan S. Connell
The Odyssey by Homer, translated by Robert Fagles
The Iliad by Homer, translated by Robert Fagles
The Siege at Peking by Peter Fleming
Decline and Fall of the Roman Empire, Volumes 1–6, by Edward Gibbon
Leviathan: Or the Matter, Forme, and Power of a Commonwealth Ecclesiasticall and Civil by Thomas Hobbes
1491: New Revelations of the Americas before Columbus by Charles C. Mann
Pax Britannica: A Three Volume Set (Heaven's Command, Pax Britannica, and *Farewell the Trumpets)* by James Morris
The Road to Reality: A Complete Guide to the Laws of the Universe by Roger Penrose
The Making of the Atomic Bomb by Richard Rhodes
Dark Sun: The Making of the Hydrogen Bomb by Richard Rhodes

If something goes horribly wrong at Long Now, there are alternative groups producing their own book lists, including the Survivor Library, which offers around 7,000 titles in PDF format. These are much more instructional and mostly from 19th-century texts which deal with very practical issues without the help of modern technology, such as:

The American Merino: A Treatise on the Selection, Care, Breeding and Diseases of the Merino Sheep by Stephen Powers

A complete run of the *British Bee Journal and Bee-Keepers Adviser*

Hand-Book of Dental Anatomy and Surgery by John Smith.

LUBBOCK'S 100 BEST BOOKS

The Bible
The Meditations of Marcus Aurelius
Epictetus
Aristotle's *Ethics*
Analects of Confucius
St. Hilaire's 'Le Bouddha et sa religion'
Wake's *Apostolic Fathers*
Thos. à Kempis's *Imitation of Christ*
Confessions of St. Augustine (Dr. Pusey)
The Koran (portions of)
Spinoza's *Tractatus Theologico-Politicus*
Comte's *Catechism of Positive Philosophy*
Pascal's *Pensées*
Butler's *Analogy of Religion*
Taylor's *Holy Living and Dying*
Bunyan's *Pilgrim's Progress*

Keble's *Christian Year*

Plato's *Dialogues*; at any rate, the *Apology*, *Phædo*, and *Republic*

Xenophon's *Memorabilia*

Aristotle's *Politics*

Demosthene's *De Corona*

Cicero's *De Officiis*, *De Amicitia*, and *de Senectute*

Plutarch's *Lives*

Berkeley's *Human Knowledge*

Descartes's *Discours sur la Méthode*

Locke's *On the Conduct of the Understanding*

Homer

Hesiod

Virgil

Epitomized in Talboys Wheeler's *History of India*, vols. i. and ii.:

Maha Bharata

Ramayana

The *Shahnameh*

The *Nibelungenlied*

Malory's *Morte d'Arthur*

The *Sheking*

Æschylus's *Prometheus*

Trilogy of Orestes

Sophocles's *Œdipus*

Euripides's *Medea*

Aristophanes's *The Knights* and *Clouds*

Horace

Lucretius

Chaucer's *Canterbury Tales* (Perhaps in Morris's edition; or, if
    expurgated, in C. Clarke's, or Mrs. Haweis's)

Shakespeare

Milton's *Paradise Lost*, *Lycidas*, and the shorter poems

Dante's *Divina Commedia*

Spenser's *Faerie Queen*

Dryden's *Poems*

Scott's *Poems*

Wordsworth (Mr. Arnold's selection)

Southey's *Thalaba the Destroyer, the Curse of Kehama*

Pope's *Essay on Criticism*

Essay on Man

Rape of the Lock

Burns

Byron's *Childe Harold*

Gray

Herodotus

Xenophon's *Anabasis*

Thucydides

Tacitus's *Germania*

Livy

Gibbon's *Decline and Fall*

Hume's *History of England*

Grote's *History of Greece*

Carlyle's *French Revolution*

Green's *Short History of England*

Lewes's *History of Philosophy*

Arabian Nights

Swift's *Gulliver's Travels*

Defoe's *Robinson Crusoe*

Goldsmith's *Vicar of Wakefield*

Cervante's *Don Quixote*

Boswell's *Life of Johnson*

Molière

Sheridan's *The Critic, School for Scandal*, and *The Rivals*

Carlyle's *Past and Present*
Smiles's *Self-Help*
Bacon's *Novum Organum*
Smith's *Wealth of Nations* (part of)
Mill's *Political Economy*
Cook's *Voyages*
Humboldt's *Travels*
White's *Natural History of Selborne*
Darwin's *Origin of Species*
Naturalist's *Voyage*
Mill's *Logic*
Bacon's *Essays*
Montaigne's *Essays*
Hume's *Essays*
Macaulay's *Essays*
Addison's *Essays*
Emerson's *Essays*
Burke's *Select works*
Voltaire's *Zadig*
Goethe's *Faust*, and *Autobiography*
Miss Austen's *Emma*, or *Pride and Prejudice*
Thackeray's *Vanity Fair*
Pendennis
Dicken's *Pickwick*
David Copperfield
Lytton's *Last Days of Pompeii*
George Eliot's *Adam Bede*
Kingsley's *Westward Ho!*
Scott's Novels

Wherever you look there are endless listicles of the '1,001 Novels You MUST Read Before You're 40' variety. We have the Godfather of the Best Books List to thank for setting this hare running: banker and philanthropist Sir John Lubbock (1834–1913). Though all but forgotten today, Lubbock was an important man, the MP responsible for introducing the Bank Holidays Act (1871), and as Principal of the Working Men's College in London he gave a speech in 1886 in which he listed 100 books.

'I drew up the list,' he said, which excluded living authors, 'not as that of the hundred best books, but, which is very different, of those which on the whole are perhaps best worth reading.' It was then published and became a best-seller, with a knock-on effect on the books mentioned. It is printed above, verbatim and in the order he listed the titles.

His top 100 (which appears to be more like 100-ish on close inspection) was organised by category, e.g. philosophy, travel, history, but he was wary about a 'science' section on the basis that 'science is so rapidly progressive'. Also, it is important to note that these were not personal favourites. 'As regards the Shi King and the Analects of Confucius, I must humbly confess that I do not greatly admire either; but I recommended these because they are held in the most profound veneration by the Chinese race.'

Following close on Lubbock's coat-tails was Dean of Canterbury and Marlborough Headmaster Frederic William Farrar, who wrote a series of monthly articles for *The Sunday Magazine* in 1898 along similar lines, though with rather more literature. But not everybody was a great fan of the concept. Oscar Wilde wrote to the *Pall Mall Gazette* in 1886 that a more important list would be the Worst

Hundred Books, so readers would know what to avoid. He then suggested dividing books into three classes:

BOOKS TO READ:
Cicero's *Letters*, Suetonius, Vasari's *Lives of the Painters*, the *Autobiography* of Benvenuto Cellini, Sir John Mandeville, Marco Polo, St Simon's *Memoirs*, Mommsen, and Grote's *History of Greece*.

BOOKS TO RE-READ:
Plato and Keats

BOOKS NOT TO READ AT ALL:
Thomson's *Seasons*, Rogers's *Italy*, Paley's *Evidences*, all the Fathers except St Augustine, all John Stuart Mill except the *Essay on Liberty*, all Voltaire's plays without any exception, Butler's *Analogy*, Grant's *Aristotle*, Hume's *England*, Lewes's *History of Philosophy*, all argumentative books and all books that try to prove anything.

Philip Waller in his excellent book *Writers, Readers and Reputations: Literary Life in Britain 1870–1918* writes that these kinds of 'best books' lists seem to some people like a 'chronic exercise in futility'.

SOLDIERS' READING LISTS: THE SOLACE OF LITERATURE IN THE TRENCHES

Quartered Safe Out Here by George MacDonald Fraser
Clausewitz: A Very Short Introduction by Michael Howard

Strategy by Basil H. Liddell Hart
Soldiers by Richard Holmes
The Face of Battle by John Keegan
The Prince by Niccolo Machiavelli (edited by George Bull)
Just and Unjust Wars by Michael Walzer

The Centre for Historical Analysis and Conflict Research, the British Army's think-tank, describes itself as 'tasked with informing military doctrine and force development and acting as an academic hub for the generation of soldier-scholars'. One way it does that is to produce reading lists – these are all thorough and extensive, but this shorter one is the Army Professional Reading List, which it describes as providing basic professional building blocks 'to get an understanding of the context in which you conduct your business and the unchanging nature of being a British soldier'.

A century ago, soldiers were still fighting, and still reading. In the First World War, camp-based lending libraries, often run by organisations such as the YMCA and the British Red Cross, were very popular, although an article in *War Illustrated* magazine in December 1915 ('The Solace of Literature in the Trenches') admits that mistakes had been made in supplying soldiers on active duty. 'We knitted him a Balaclava helmet to keep his head warm and omitted to provide anything to supply the inside of his brain.'

Books were certainly a popular commodity in the trenches, useful aids during the long periods of inaction and a means of passing the time, as well as taking men's minds off the horrors unfolding around them. Particularly popular were works by Rudyard Kipling, John Buchan (especially *The Thirty-Nine Steps*) and the hugely prolific Nat Gould, who specialised in horse-racing stories. W.W. Jacobs's work offered some humour and there was also considerable demand for Jane Austen's novels. Her work was also used as an early form of bibliotherapy for soldiers suffering from shell shock.

Adventure and crime stories such as those featuring Sherlock Holmes and Sexton Blake were also on the most-read list, and Conan Doyle brought the great detective out of retirement in 'The Last Bow' specifically to help the war effort. Sentimental stories were well liked too, especially ones with VC in the title, such as Ruby M. Ayres's heroic romance *Richard Chatterton, VC*. Chatterton starts the novel as a louche slacker spending all his time at his club. His failure to enlist loses him his fiancée, but eventually he does sign up and becomes a changed man after various astonishingly brave incidents and wounds (and of course he wins his girl back). It was published in 1916, and around 70,000 copies were printed by the end of the war.

One key element in choosing what to read was simply the size of the books – large tomes were not sufficiently portable, so consequently Penguins and other pocket-sized editions were highly prized. For this reason, Shakespeare's plays were read individually rather than in collected editions. However, ownership was not always necessary. A Captain Corbett-Smith is said to have read *A Christmas Carol* to his troops in the trenches.

In his *Books in Camp, Trench and Hospital* written in 1917, Theodore Wesley Koch investigated first-hand what soldiers were reading. As well as sensational fiction, he noted that poetry was also in demand, especially *Hundred*

Best Poems anthologies, plus books on handicrafts, maps and even Bradshaw's railway timetables. 'A book must not be too formidable or sombre to look at,' he wrote. 'It's like a cyclist with a long hill in front of him – the sight makes him tired.' Officers, he noted, went for the more expensive six-shilling novels and 'lighter biographies'. He lists three in particular:

Garibaldi and the Thousand by George M. Trevelyan
Beatrice D'Este, Duchess of Milan, 1475–1497: A Study of the Renaissance by Julia Cartwright
Portraits and Sketches by Edmund Gosse

UNIVERSITY READING LISTS

The Elements of Style by William Strunk
The Republic by Plato
The Communist Manifesto by Karl Marx
Biology by Neil Campbell
Frankenstein by Mary Wollstonecraft Shelley
Ethics by Aristotle
Leviathan by Thomas Hobbes
The Prince by Niccolo Machiavelli
Oedipus by Sophocles
Hamlet by William Shakespeare

If you like lists of books, there is no finer way of losing hours of your life to the internet than by heading towards the Open Syllabus Project at explorer.opensyllabusproject.org.

This enormous undertaking aims to bring together in one database all college and university syllabuses in the USA, UK, Canada, Australia and New Zealand. At the moment it holds about 1.1 million, mostly from the last fifteen years. Overall, it provides an intriguing picture of which books are moulding our students' thoughts and lives. Or as the *Washington Post* puts it, 'What Ivy League students are reading that you aren't'. The top ten most-assigned titles are listed above.

One of the beauties of the site is that there are various filters you can put in place to drill down. So using 'History' + 'United Kingdom' results in:

Orientalism by Edward Said
What is History? by E.H. Carr
The End of the British Empire: The Historical Debate by John
    Darwin
In Defence of History by Richard Evans
The Making of the English Working Class by E.P. Thompson
The Pursuit of History by John Tosh
The Communist Manifesto by Karl Marx
Hope and Glory: Britain, 1900–2000
British Imperialism, 1688–2000
History in Practice by L.J. Jordanova

And here's what 'English' + 'Mississippi' looks like:

The Open Boat by Stephen Crane
The Love Song of J. Alfred Prufrock by T.S. Eliot
Death of a Salesman by Arthur Miller
Deliverance by James Dickey

A Streetcar Named Desire by Tennessee Williams
The Awakening by Kate Chopin
Hamlet by William Shakespeare
Invisible Man by Ralph Ellison
The Sound and the Fury by William Faulkner
Gimpel the Fool by Isaac Bashevis Singer

In general, writing guides such as *The Elements of Style* and textbooks (e.g. *Biology* by Neil Campbell) do well in many lists. So does, perhaps somewhat surprisingly, *The Communist Manifesto*, the result of it being included in numerous disciplines including history, sociology and politics. It also throws up some unusual results. If you try 'English' + 'University of Oxford', Wolfgang Amadeus Mozart's String Quartet number 14 in G Major K387 comes in at an impressive number 7.

There are also other ways the data can be analysed. The Open Syllabus team point to TIME magazine's mistake in adding Evelyn Waugh to its list of the '100 Most-Read Female Writers in College Classes' as perhaps the result of the author of *Decline and Fall* being 'one of the losers in literature canon change, and that as a result very few people under 40 have read him or, accordingly, been corrected on his gender during college'.

Incidentally, the top ten on TIME's list were (most-read first):

Kate L. Turabian
Diana Hacker
Toni Morrison
Jane Austen

Virginia Woolf
Mary Wollstonecraft Shelley
Elaine Nicpon Marieb
Charlotte Perkins Gilman
Mary Wollstonecraft
George Eliot

Ideas specialists TED.com have put together a slightly more anecdotal list of which classic books are assigned to students in countries around the world, in the way that *Lord of the Flies* is read in the UK or *To Kill a Mockingbird* in the USA. This includes:

Albania – *Kronikë në gur* (*Chronicle in Stone*) by Ismail Kadare
Bosnia; Serbia – *Na drini ćuprija* (*The Bridge on the Drina*) by Ivo Andrić
Brazil – *Morte e vida Severina* (*The Death of a Severino*) by João Cabral de Melo Neto
Finland – *Seitsemän veljestä* (*Seven Brothers*) by Aleksis Kiv
Italy – *I Promessi Sposi* (*The Betrothed*) by Alessandro Manzoni
Philippines – *Noli Me Tangere* (*Touch Me Not*) by Jose Rizal
Vietnam – *Truyên Kiêu* (*The Tale of Kiêu*) by Nguyễn Du

PREMIER LEAGUE FOOTBALLERS' FAVOURITE READS

Topsy and Tim by Jean Adamson and Gareth Adamson (Brede Hangeland)
Paddington by Michael Bond (Dean Hammond)
Charlie and the Chocolate Factory by Roald Dahl (Paddy McNair)

Danny, the Champion of the World by Roald Dahl (Kyle Bartley)

James and the Giant Peach by Roald Dahl (Russ Martin, Rene Gilmartin and James Ward-Prowse)

A Very Special Mouse and Vole by Joyce Dunbar (Darren Randolph)

Demolition Dad by Phil Earle (Brad Guzan)

The Keeper: The Unguarded Story of Tim Howard, Young Readers' Edition by Tim Howard (Leighton Baines)

The Three Little Pigs, Ladybird edition (Héctor Bellerín)

Kensuke's Kingdom by Michael Morpurgo (Duncan Watmore)

Harry Potter and the Philosopher's Stone by J.K. Rowling (Charlie Adam, Freddie Woodman, Ryan Mason and Adam Bogdan)

Where the Wild Things Are by Maurice Sendak (Boaz Myhill and Ruben Loftus-Cheek)

Green Eggs and Ham by Dr Seuss (Patrick Roberts)

Oxford Reading Tree Read With Biff, Chip, and Kipper: First Stories (Callum Wilson)

Since the 2002/03 football season, the National Literacy Trust has run its Premier League Reading Stars programme, inviting top-flight footballers from each of the leading clubs in the UK to pick their favourite books and encourage children, especially boys, to read. Above are their favourite children's titles from the 2015/16 season (in brackets the footballers who chose them).

The scheme certainly works. Nearly two-thirds of children who take part say that seeing Premier League footballers reading and talking about books made them want to read more, while there is a 50 per cent increase in the number of children who enjoy reading at the end of the programme. Three out of four pupils' reading levels increased significantly, as did their enjoyment and confidence. More than half of those who take part then go on to visit a library as a result.

'You might not realise it, but education is very important for a footballer,' says Arsenal's Héctor Bellerín. 'As an academy player you need to study until you are 18. And you never know, you may have an injury so it's important to have a good education. Like in football, don't ever give up. If you haven't found the right book for you, keep going, you will.'

Choices in previous years have included Muhammad Ali's autobiography *The Soul of a Butterfly* (Bacary Sagna), *Lord of the Flies* (Boaz Myhill) and *The Iliad*, chosen by goalkeeper Rob Green. 'Reading is such a big part of all our lives, everyone should try to make a bit of time each day to read more,' he says. 'You should never be scared of a book either. Reading classics like *The Iliad* might seem daunting, but if you take your time, they really are interesting to read and you gain such a lot from trying them.' Indeed, in previous years the books have included *Jonathan Strange and Mr Norrell* by Susanna Clarke (Darren Bent) and *The Diary of a Young Girl* by Anne Frank (Ruud Van Nistelrooy).

And of course the football element can appeal to authors too. Darren Shan was delighted when his book *Zom-B Angels* was picked by Tottenham Hotspur's central defender Jan Vertonghen. 'I was particularly pleased about this choice,' he said, 'as this is the team I support!'

DYLAN THOMAS ON ROBERT BROWNING

'Summum Bonum'

'Confessions'

'A Likeness'

'Porphyria's Lover'

'Soliloquy of the Spanish Cloister'

'My Last Duchess'

'Johannes Agricola in Meditation'

'A Light Woman'

'The Lost Mistress'

'Evelyn Hope'

'May and Death'

'Never the Time and the Place'

These twelve poems by Robert Browning were written down by Dylan Thomas around 1947 on the back of an unstamped envelope that he intended to send to Osbert Sitwell but never did. Nobody knows what they represent, though it appears likely they were for a radio programme or public reading.

J.P. MORGAN'S ANNUAL SUMMER READING LIST

The Third Wave: An Entrepreneur's Vision of the Future by Steve Case

Grit: The Power of Passion and Perseverance by Angela Duckworth

From Silk to Silicon: The Story of Globalization Through Ten

Extraordinary Lives by Jeffrey E Garten
Originals: How Non-Conformists Move the World by
    Adam Grant
*The Sleep Revolution: Transforming Your Life, One Night at
    a Time* by Arianna Huffington
Lab Girl by Hope Jahren
Hamilton: The Revolution by Lin-Manuel Miranda and Jeremy
    McCarter
Map: Exploring the World by Phaidon Editors
Clementine: The Life of Mrs Winston Churchill by Sonia Purnell
*The End of Average: How We Succeed in a World That Values
    Sameness* by Todd Rose

Releasing an annual reading list or running your own
book club is becoming a *de rigueur* part of being a celebrity, not just among the literati but increasingly among
businessmen too. Philanthropist and Microsoft founder
Bill Gates is one of those who feels an urge to share his
favourites, which in 2016 were:

The Grid by Gretchen Bakke
The Myth of the Strong Leader by Archie Brown
Shoe Dog by Phil Knight
The Gene by Siddhartha Mukherjee
String Theory by David Foster Wallace

This differs slightly from his summer reading list, which
included *Seveneves* by Neal Stephenson, *How Not to be Wrong*
by Jordan Ellenberg and *Sapiens: A Brief History of Mankind* by
Yuval Noah Harari. The reasons for his choices are fairly
straightforward. They are 'simply ones that I loved, made

me think in new ways, and kept me up reading long past when I should have gone to sleep'.

Banking giant J.P. Morgan is so keen on reading lists that it has been producing an annual summer edition of its top ten picks since 1999. The most recent titles – listed top – were whittled down from nearly 450 works of non-fiction nominated by staff from its offices around the world on the basis of timeliness, quality, author credentials, innovation and global appeal.

'We work with an incredibly dynamic and diverse group of clients and everything we do reflects that unique perspective,' says Darin Oduyoye, Chief Communications Officer. 'The summer reading list is our effort to extend the dialogue beyond the bread and butter of our business to help clients discover new ideas, new people and new thinking.'

Goldman Sachs has been offering something similar chosen by its managing directors and partners since 2015. Its 'Back-to-School Reading List' offers autumnal recommendations 'for every age and career stage'. Indeed, its CEO Lloyd Blankfein once told an interviewer that younger readers would be better off reading history rather than economics books. 'You can see that all these people who did really great things failed six times, or didn't get going until they were much older,' he said. 'I think that's much more instructive and educational.'

GS tantalisingly releases its lists a bit at a time and they are considerably longer than J.P. Morgan's. Here is its first one for 2016, offering a much wider mix of genres, while still including a Churchill. Only one title on its final longlist – which included *Inverting the Pyramid: the History of*

Football Tactics, by Jonathan Wilson – overlapped with J.P. Morgan's, Angela Duckworth on Grit:

Half of a Yellow Sun by Chimamanda Ngozi Adichie
Seinfeldia: How a Show about Nothing Changed Everything by
   Jennifer Keishin Armstrong
Between the World and Me by Ta-Nehisi Coates
Churchill: A Life by Martin Gilbert
Homegoing by Yaa Gyasi
*Black Wealth, White Wealth: A New Perspective on Racial
   Inequality* by Melvin L. Oliver and Thomas Shapiro
*The Signal and the Noise: Why So Many Predictions Fail – But
   Some Don't* by Nate Silver
The Healthy Workplace by Leigh Stringer
A Little Life by Hanya Yanagihara

Chapter Two
ON THE MOVE

BOOKCROSSING'S MOST REGISTERED

Half of a Yellow Sun by Chimamanda Ngozi Adichie
Case Histories by Kate Atkinson
The Blind Assassin by Margaret Atwood
A Life Like Other People's by Alan Bennett
The Spy Who Came In from the Cold by John le Carré
Killing Floor by Lee Child
The Curious Incident of the Dog in the Night-Time by Mark Haddon
The Reluctant Fundamentalist by Mohsin Hamid
New Selected Poems by Seamus Heaney
Rachel's Holiday by Marian Keyes
Love in the Time of Cholera by Gabriel García Márquez
Life of Pi by Yann Martel
A Fine Balance by Rohinton Mistry
Cloud Atlas by David Mitchell
One Day by David Nicholls
Northern Lights by Philip Pullman
All Quiet on the Western Front by Erich Maria Remarque
Toast by Nigel Slater
The Prime of Miss Jean Brodie by Muriel Spark
Fingersmith by Sarah Waters

BookCrossing, a fine cocktail of old media and new social networking site, describes itself as the world's library. Essentially, readers register a book – the top twenty favourites are listed above – then release it into the wild where anybody can pick it up, read it, comment on it online, then leave it somewhere else. There are more than 11 million books on the move in more than 130 countries and well over 1.5 million Bookcrossers reading them.

The brainchild of Ron Hornbaker, Ron's wife Kaori and co-founders Bruce and Heather Pedersen, the site has been up and running since 2001. 'Our community is changing the world,' they say, 'and touching lives one book at a time.' At the time of writing, the top five BookCrossing countries are USA, Germany, the United Kingdom, the Netherlands and Finland. The ten most-travelled books (again at the time of writing, as the lists are constantly changing) are:

Bill Bryson's African Diary by Bill Bryson
Apocalisse 23 by Michele Fabbri
A Passage to India by E.M. Forster
Der weisse Neger Wumbaba by Axel Hacke and Michael Sowa
Der seltsame Bücherfreund (Hoffnung's Constant Readers) by
    Gerard Hoffnung
Little Johnnie and the Naughty Boat People by Christopher
    Milne
Mrs Biddlebox by Linda Smith
Was ich dir zum Geburtstag wünsche – Das Buch zu
    Patschoulis 90 by Ellen Sonntag
Kamasutra der Frösche by Tomi Ungerer
Ojalá Jane Fonda nos ilumine by Marcelo Juan Valenti

Londoners caught short without decent reading matter can also make use of the Books on the Underground scheme, which has put/hidden more than 15,000 free new and used books around the Underground network (on trains, seats, signs, ticket counters) since 2012, a figure which is growing by around 150 a week. So successful has it been that there are now satellite sites in New York (Books on the Subway), Washington (Books on the Metro), Chicago (Books on the L) and Sydney (Books on the Rail).

All genres are represented in these 'Books on' schemes, from poetry to colouring-in books. Here is a typical list, from October 2016, of books you may have sat next to on the tube in London:

The Tattooist by Louise Black
Pavement: Thoughts of a Serial Killer by Richard Butchins
The Hitchcock Murders by Gavin Collinson
Pirates by Greg Cummings
The Wrong Train by Jeremy deQuidt
The Secret by Katerina Diamond
Tigeropolis: Beyond the Deep Forest by R.D. Dikstra
My Beautiful England by Michelle Flatley
Who Are You? by Elizabeth Forbes
Moskva by Jack Grimwood
Love You Dead by Peter James
The Judas Scar by Amanda Jennings
The Fairy's Tale by F.D. Lee
Drinks with Dead Poets by Glyn Maxwell
Dark River Melody by M.D. Murphy
The Secret Wife by Gill Paul
Twin Truths by Shelan Rodger

Wicked Game by Eve Seymour
Game Over by Eve Seymour
Lockwood & Co: The Screaming Staircase by Jonathan Stroud
Tall Oaks by Christopher Whitaker
The Blackheath Seance by Alan L. Williams

BOOKS LEFT BEHIND IN HOTELS

1. *Fifty Shades Freed* by E.L. James
2. *Bared To You* by Sylvia Day
3. *The Marriage Bargain* by Jennifer Probst
4. *Gone Girl* by Gillian Flynn
5. *The Casual Vacancy* by J.K. Rowling
6. *Fifty Shades of Grey* by E.L. James
7. *Reflected In You* by Sylvia Day
8. *My Time* by Bradley Wiggins
9. *Entwined With You* by Sylvia Day
10. *Fifty Shades Darker* by E.L. James
11. *My Story* by Cheryl Cole
12. *The Marriage Trap* by Jennifer Probst
13. *Camp David* by David Walliams
14. *Call The Midwife: A True Story of the East End in the 1950s* by Jennifer Worth
15. *Before I Go To Sleep* by S.J. Watson
16. *The Marriage Mistake* by Jennifer Probst
17. *The Racketeer* by John Grisham
18. *The Carrier* by Sophie Hannah
19. *Oh Dear Silvia* by Dawn French
20. *The Great Gatsby* by F. Scott Fitzgerald

One of the increasing additions to luxury hotels in recent years has been an impressive library. The Library Hotel in New York has gone so far as to theme each of its ten guest-room floors on a single category in the Dewey Decimal System, with each of the sixty rooms featuring a collection of books focusing on a topic within the category to which it belongs.

But what about the books that arrive with their owners? Not all books get to go home with them, many parting ways during overnight stays or en route on trains and planes. The Travelodge chain reports an annual list of 'left behinds' in all their hotels, with books and Kindles both featuring in the top ten. The lists include books which have been genuinely forgotten, simply dumped, or deliberately left behind for other readers. Indeed, this final reason is the main accession procedure for the library of the President of the United States' official guest residence Blair House in Washington D.C., which holds around 1,500 volumes left behind as diplomatic gifts by foreign delegations who have stayed there over the years.

Travelodge has also drilled down to reveal which titles top the table, with trilogies making a particularly strong showing in the most recent list, featured above (the Fifty Shades threesome – which was most frequently left behind in Travelodge's Yorkshire hotels – also rides high in Oxfam's list of most-donated books, as does the work of Dan Brown). In recent years Stieg Larsson's Millennium trilogy has also been a consistently good performer.

As in previous years, there is much more fiction (especially of the erotic/romance variety) than non-fiction on the list compiled from the 22,648 books left behind. It also continues to chart the growing decline of celebrity biographies on the list since it was topped in 2010 by *Simon Cowell: The Unauthorised Biography* by Chas Newkey-Burden.

Previous number ones have included Katie Price's autobiography *Pushed to the Limit*, Piers Morgan's *Don't You Know Who I Am?* and *The Blair Years* by Alastair Campbell, which topped the first-ever list in 2007 (a year which also saw a huge number of Mills & Boon and English-language phrasebooks). Children's books rarely feature, although in 2012 *Diary of a Wimpy Kid* made the 14th spot, and there are also appearances for the Hunger Games books and the Harry Potter series. In 2012, a sports book was found in all fifty-seven London Travelodges during the Olympics.

Of course books also go walkabout elsewhere. More than 80,000 books, documents and cards were left behind on London's public transport network between 2015 and 2016, while Virgin Atlantic's cabin crews compiled a list of ditched titles over the Christmas 2011 period which – interestingly – put Richard Branson's *Screw Business As Usual* at number 8. The full top ten was:

1. *The Way I See It* by Alan Sugar
2. *Glorious: My World, Football and Me* by Paul Gascoigne
3. *Santa Baby* by Katie Price
4. *The World of Downton Abbey* by Jessica Fellowes
5. *I Heart Vegas* by Lindsey Kelk
6. *Twisting My Melon* by Shaun Ryder
7. *May I Have Your Attention, Please?* by James Corden
8. *Screw Business as Usual* by Richard Branson
9. *An Idiot Abroad: Travel Diaries* by Karl Pilkington
10. *The Help* by Kathryn Stockett

Lord Sugar's book was found most often on routes from London to New York, Tokyo and Shanghai.

SCOTT'S DISCOVERY LIBRARY

Cook's Voyages of Discovery by John Barrow
Voyages of Foxe and James by Miller Christy
First Crossing of Spitzbergen by Sir Martin Conway
With Ski and Sledge over Arctic Glaciers by Sir Martin Conway
Narrative of Voyage to South Seas by Charles M. Goodridge
Danish Arctic Expeditions by C.C.A. Gosch
Handbook of Arctic Discoveries by A.W. Greely
Three Years of Arctic Service by A.W. Greely
Through Arctic Lapland by Cutliffe Hyne
German Arctic Expedition by Captain Karl Koldewey
Fate of Franklin, and his Discoveries by F.L. McClintock
Arctic Voyage of H.M.S. Resolute by G.F. McDougall
Polar Reconnaissance by Captain A.H. Markham
Northward Ho! By Captain A.H. Markham
Franklin's Footsteps by Sir Clements R. Markham
Voyages of William Baffin by Sir Clements R. Markham
Naturalist's Notes on H.M.S. Challenger by H.N. Moseley
Castaway on the Auckland Isles by Thomas Musgrave
First Crossing of Greenland by Fridtjof Nansen
Voyage to the Polar Seas: 'Alert' and 'Discovery' by Sir G.S. Nares
North-West Passage (Third Voyage) by W.E. Parry
Austrian Arctic Voyage by Julius Payer
Voyage to the Southern Seas by Sir James C. Ross
North Georgia Gazette: 'Hecla' and 'Griper' Expedition by
  Captain Edward Sabine

Arctic Regions by W. Scoresby

Under the Rays of Aurora Borealis by Sophus Tromholt

When you are planning a major expedition, the first 'must-have' to include on your packing list is naturally thousands of books.

On Captain Robert Falcon Scott's *Discovery* expedition of 1901–04, as well as plenty of food and warm clothes, he also put together what became the impressive National Antarctic Expedition Library. This onboard collection even warranted its own catalogue, a 34-page pamphlet divided into sections including 'Biographical', 'Essays and Philosophical', 'Historical', 'Travel', 'Fiction', 'Poetical', 'Magazines', 'Reference', 'Scientific' and 'Expeditions'. Each section was arranged alphabetically by author and includes the precise location of each book – in Scott's own cabin, the officers' cabins, the ward room mess-cabin for commissioned officers, and the seamen's mess deck.

So we can tell that Scott kept hold of all the Sir Walter Scotts and a good chunk of the travel and maritime books. *Alice's Adventures in Wonderland* and *Through the Looking Glass* were on the mess deck, as were the popular hunting novels of Major George John Whyte-Melville, and the thirty-five volumes of *Punch* magazine. The Dickens – including *A Christmas Carol* – were in the Ward Room, and Lieutentant Michael Barne had Jerome K. Jerome's *Three Men in a Boat* in his own quarters. Expedition members had their own personal Bibles.

As only around twenty were printed, the catalogue is itself a rarity and an expensive buy when it does come up for auction occasionally, but happily the Antarctic Circle group of scholars has put a copy up for public viewing online at www.antarctic-circle.org/discoverylibrary.pdf. The list above is of the travel section of the polar books (Arctic and Antarctic) in the National Antarctic Expedition Library.

Of course Scott was not the only explorer who could have made good use of an e-reader's capabilities. While Martin Frobisher probably had only about a dozen books on his first Arctic voyage in 1576, Sir John Franklin's ships *Erebus* and *Terror* 300 years later had a combined library of around 3,000. Sir Ernest Shackleton also made room en route to Antarctica on his ship *Endurance* for plenty of books. A photo taken in March 1915 by photographer Frank Hurley has been analysed by the Royal Geographical Society and digitalisation experts to reveal that his own cabin bookshelf contained the following:

The Northwest Passage by Roald Amundsen
Pros and Cons: A Newspaper Reader's and Debater's Guide to the Leading Controversies of the Day by J.B. Askew
Perch of the Devil by Gertrude Atherton
The Barrier by Rex Beach
Thou Fool by J.J. Bell
Cassell's Book of Quotations by W. Gurney Benham
The Grand Babylon Hotel by Arnold Bennett
Oddsfish by Robert Hugh Benson
The Brassbounder by David Bone
The Reader's Handbook of Famous Names in Fiction, Allusions, References, Proverbs, Plots, Stories, and Poems by Ebenezer Cobham Brewer
Journal of HMS Enterprise by Sir Richard Collinson

Almayer's Folly by Joseph Conrad
The Brothers Karamazov by Fyodor Dostoyevsky
Five Years of my Life by Alfred Dreyfuss
The Woman's View by Herbert Flowerdew
Potash and Perlmutter by Montague Glass
Three Years of Arctic Service by Adolphus Greely
Seven Short Plays by Lady Gregory
Pip: A Romance of Youth by Ian Hey
Raffles by E.W. Hornung
United States Grinnell Expedition by Dr Elisha Kane
The Morals of Marcus Ordeyne by William J. Locke
Round the Horn Before the Mast by A. Basil Lubbock
The Threshold of the Unknown Region by Clements Markham
The Witness for the Defence by A.E.W. Mason
The Voyage of the Fox in Arctic Seas by Francis McClintock
Voyage to the Polar Sea by George Nares
Manual of English Grammar and Composition by John Nesfield
Voyage of the Vega by Baron Nils Adolf Erik Nordenskiöld
The Case of Miss Elliott by Emmuska Orczy
World's End by Amelie Rives
The Rescue of Greely by Commander Winfield Scott Schley
Plays: Pleasant and Unpleasant by George Bernard Shaw
Poetical Works of Percy Bysshe Shelley
Monsieur de Rochefort by H. De Vere Stacpoole
The Message of Fate by Louis Tracy
Encyclopaedia Britannica
Whitaker's Almanac
Various dictionaries

DESERT ISLAND DISCS: THE BOOKS

Divine Comedy by Dante Alighieri
Pride and Prejudice by Jane Austen
A History of the English-Speaking Peoples by Winston Churchill
Robinson Crusoe by Daniel Defoe
The History of the Decline and Fall of the Roman Empire by
  Edward Gibbon
The Wind in the Willows by Kenneth Grahame
Iliad/Odyssey by Homer
À la recherche du temps perdu by Marcel Proust
Lord of the Rings by J.R.R. Tolkien
War and Peace by Leo Tolstoy

Guests on *Desert Island Discs* have been choosing their favourite records since Roy Plomley first came up with the format for the radio show in 1942. Not much has changed since then, although one major introduction was allowing the castaway to also pick a book – the first one was actor Henry Kendall in 1951 (he chose *Who's Who in the Theatre*, which was also picked by Roy Plomley himself when Eamonn Andrews cast him away in 1958).

This is the list of the top ten choices, which could be stretched to eleven if you include the general 'dictionary'. It should arguably also include the complete Shakespeare and the Bible which everybody is given, although various castaways have refused the Bible (Michael Mansfield QC, David Walliams, opera director David MacVicar, Tariq Ali and mountain climber Joe Simpson all wanted a Bible-less existence). Showjumper Harvey Smith (1971) also refused to pick a book, explaining that he never read, while

George Clooney (2003) selected *War and Peace* 'as there may not be toilet paper, and that's a huge book'. Foreign correspondent Anthony Grey (1969) slightly bent the rules by asking for the book stall in Victoria station as his luxury.

Aaron Hicklin, owner of the One Grand bookshop in Narrowsbury, New York, has taken the concept a stage further. He asks well-known writers, artists and creative minds to choose ten books they would take to a desert island and then stocks his shelves accordingly (sometimes this causes problems – he had some difficulty in tracking down Sir Thomas Browne's 1658 *Urn Burial* selected by artist Raymond Pettibon). As an example, here are novelist Jay McInerney's ten desert island best:

Emma by Jane Austen
Lost Illusions by Honoré de Balzac
Death on the Installment Plan by Louis-Ferdinand Céline
The Great Gatsby by F. Scott Fitzgerald
The Sun Also Rises by Ernest Hemingway
Ulysses by James Joyce
A Sport and a Pastime by James Salter
A Handful of Dust by Evelyn Waugh
The Custom of the Country by Edith Wharton
The Code of the Woosters by P.G. Wodehouse

Children's books are not frequently picked on Desert Island Discs, but in 1993 the Reading and Language Information Centre at the University of Reading contacted various children's authors asking them which books they would give to children aged 8–10 if they were marooned on a desert island. Shirley Hughes picked *Fairy Tales of the*

British Isles and Treasure Island by R.L. Stevenson (the most popular choice overall), Anthony Browne went for *Alice's Adventures in Wonderland*, and Michael Foreman for *The Wind in the Willows*.

NAPOLEON'S TRAVELLING LIBRARY

Theatre de Corneille, 5 vols
Theatre de Racine, 4 vols
Theatre de Voltaire, 5 vols
Ourves de Boileau, 1 vol
Fables de La Fontaine, 2 vols
Contes de La Fontaine, 2 vols
La Pucelle d'Orleans, par Voltaire, 1 vol
Ourves de Gresset, 1 vol
Ourves de Bernis, 1 vol
Ourves de Vergier et Grecourt, 1 vol
Ourves de Molier, 7 vols
Ourves de Piron, 2 vols
Letters a Emilie sur la Mythologies par Demoustier, 3 vols
Grandeur des Romains par Montesquieu, 1 vol
Discours sur L'History Universelle par Bossuet, 3 vols
Histoire de Gil Blas par Lesage, 5 vols
Les Amours de Daphnis et Chloe, 1 vol
Histoire du Petit Jehan de Saintre et de Gerard de Nevers
   par Trefsau, 1 vol
Memoires de Grammont, 2 vols
Telemaque, 1 vol

Napoleon was arguably the best-read emperor the world has ever seen. As a young man he particularly enjoyed Plutarch's *Lives of the Noble Grecians and Romans*, and in exile on Saint Helena one of his favourites was *Paul et Virginie* by Jacques-Henri Bernardin de Saint-Pierre. But he was also keen not to be separated from reading matter while on campaigns, so wisely commissioned various travel libraries which were put together by his personal librarian Antoine-Alexandre Barbier. These contained hundreds of volumes and covered military tactics, history, geography and religion as well as novels, poetry and plays.

In addition to these, he also ordered a smaller, more manageable travel library in a wooden box resembling a large book measuring around 15 by 10 inches, stocked with French classics in appropriately bespoke smaller format (see list above). Each volume was bound in roan leather and tooled in gilt. As well as the ones for his own use on campaigns, he gave sets to his generals, with the number of volumes varying from around a dozen up to fifty.

Travelling libraries had been popular for centuries before Boney. Henry VIII travelled with chests full of books as he wandered around England, and Francis I had a similar arrangement in France, with Appian, Justinus and Thucydides among its featured authors. Around 100 years later, English antiquarian and MP William Hakewill (1574–1655) commissioned several travelling libraries as gifts for friends and patrons. Inside the booklike structure were three shelves of miniature-edition classics bound in vellum and with gold-tooling on the spines, which also each feature a flower. The cover of every volume features a golden angel holding a scroll bearing 'Gloria Deo'.

Several still survive, including one in the British Library which was owned by Master of the Rolls Sir Julius Caesar (1558–1636) and another in the Brotherton College at the Library of the University of Leeds. There is a painted catalogue of the contents on the inside 'front cover' – one shelf for Theology and Philosophy, one for History, and one for Poetry – including works by Cicero, Julius Caesar (no relation), Seneca, Horace, Virgil and Ovid.

One of the most interesting features of these travelling libraries is their size, which appears very familiar to modern eyes – Stella Butler, University Librarian and Keeper of the Brotherton Collection, describes them as 'essentially a 17th-century e-book reader'.

Now somewhat out of fashion, travelling libraries are still with us. Tom Stoppard travels with a book satchel from New York luggage specialist T. Anthony which is about the size of a bread bin and can hold up to around a dozen books. As an example, on a trip to New York in 2007, his packing list included:

50 Mathematical Ideas You Really Need to Know by Tony Crilly
Ethics by G.E. Moore
Blackwater by Jeremy Scahill
Gravity's Rainbow by Thomas Pynchon

NERD: THE UNITED STATES NAVY'S E-READER

Ender's Game by Orson Scott Card
The Amazing Adventures of Kavalier & Clay by Michael Chabon

Robinson Crusoe by Daniel Defoe

Bossypants by Tina Fey

The Odyssey by Homer

The Stand by Stephen King

Into The Wild by Jon Krakauer

The Girl With the Dragon Tattoo by Stieg Larsson

To Kill a Mockingbird by Harper Lee

The Lion, The Witch and the Wardrobe by C.S. Lewis

A Game of Thrones by George R.R. Martin

1776 by David McCullough

The Immortal Life of Henrietta Lack by Rebecca Skloot

The Lord of the Rings by J.R.R. Tolkien

The King James Bible

The Quran (Koran)

The Book of Mormon

Most of the 18 titles in the Chief of Naval Operations'
   Professional Reading Programme

Various works by William Shakespeare, Jane Austen, James
   Joyce, Walt Whitman and Samuel Taylor Coleridge

Commercially available e-readers are not suitable for the submarines of the United States Navy because of various security and technology issues. But sailors like to read and there is limited storage for books, so the solution is the Navy e-Reader Device – known rather unfortunately as the NeRD – produced in conjunction with audiobook technology specialists Findaway.

Each submarine has five NeRDs, produced at a cost of $3,000 each, and with familiar basic features such as adjustable typefaces and sizes, as well as a carrying case. Every NeRD can hold around 300 books but has no internet capability, no camera and no removable storage. The list of classics, modern fiction, history and professional development is constantly reviewed to ensure it appeals to men and women, for example adding more books with female protagonists to the original science-fiction list (the above is a list of titles which have already been chosen). Hunt for *Red October* is not one of the choices.

'It is a definite hit with the submarine force,' says Kevin Rollert, chief of the boat USS *Jacksonville*. 'During at-sea time there is routinely a five-person waitlist. The material is what today's sailors want to read and is one of the most popular morale items on board.'

After the successful submarine trial, the NeRD has now been released to the surface fleet including minesweepers, destroyers, frigates, cruisers and hospital ships.

Chapter Three

IN THE LIBRARY

US LIGHT HOUSE ESTABLISHMENT LIBRARY BOX 141

The Reflections of a Lonely Man by A.C.M.

Pictures Every Child Should Know: A Selection of the World's Art Masterpieces for Young People by Dolores Bacon

Farm Festivals by Will Carleton

Farm Ballads by Will Carleton

Farm Legends by Will Carleton

City Festivals by Will Carleton

My Apingi Kingdom: With Life in the Great Sahara, and Sketches of the Chase by Paul Belloni du Chaillu

The Pilot: A Tale of the Sea by James Fenimore Cooper

Sailors' Knots by Cyrus Lawrence Day

Tuscan Republics by Bella Duffy

Madame Thérèse by Émile Erckmann and Alexandre Chatrian

Hoosier Lyrics by Eugene Field

British India by Robert Watson Frazer

Mosses from an Old Manse by Nathaniel Hawthorne

The Professor at the Breakfast-Table by Oliver Wendell Holmes Sr

A Moral Antipathy by Oliver Wendell Holmes

Toilers of the Sea by Victor Hugo

The Little Colonel's Holidays by Annie Fellows Johnston

The Phantom Rickshaw and Other Tales by Rudyard Kipling

The Navy in the Civil War Volume XVI (The Gulf and Inland Waters) by A.T. Mahan

Reveries of a Bachelor or A Book of the Heart by Donald Grant Mitchell

Voyage with Columbus: A Story of Two Boys Who Sailed with the Great Admiral in 1492 by Frederick Ober

An Adventure of the North by Gilbert Parker

Cromwell's Own by Arthur Patterson

Quincy Adams Sawyer by Charles Felton Pidgin

Driven from Sea to Sea: Or, Just a Campin' by Charles Cyrel Post

Century Readings for a Course in English Literature edited by J.F. Pyre, Karl Young and J.W. Cunliffe

Works of James Whitcomb Riley

The Magnetic North by Elizabeth Robins

Wonders of Nature; Described By Great Writers (including Victor Hugo, Charles Dickens, John Keats, William Makepeace Thackeray, Hans Christian Andersen) edited by Esther Singleton

Lighthouse keepers and their families in the 19th century needed something to combat the boredom of their isolated working and living conditions. From the late 1870s, a network of portable libraries grew up. These were sturdy wooden cases that contained up to sixty books and magazines on several shelves and were passed between lighthouses around the United States.

Each case had a list of contents and details about which lighthouses it had visited, and for how long, stuck to the inside of the doors. Number 739, for example, made its maiden voyage in 1898 to Eagle Bluff lighthouse in Door County, Wisconsin, then took in numerous other locations including Wind Point, Waugoshance and Cana Island, and finally came to rest at Point Betsie, Michigan in 1912.

The libraries were stocked thanks to donations from private individuals and groups such as the religious organisation the American Seamen's Friend Society. At its peak, the highly popular service provided hundreds of these portable libraries. The list above is a typical selection, now on permanent display in the Piedras Blancas lighthouse in San Simeon.

It features quite an eclectic range of titles, from tear-jerking Victorian melodrama (Quincy Adams Sawyer, *The Little Colonel's Holidays*), to more heavyweight fare (*Madame Thérèse* is set during the French Revolution and focuses on the concepts of justice and equality). Poetry is represented by regional dialect specialists Whitcomb Riley (*Little Orphant Annie*) and Eugene Field (*Wynken, Blynken, and Nod*) as well as the work of Will Carleton, whose subject choice and approach resembles that of Robert Burns. Unsurprisingly, there are various titles that will strike a chord with workers in remote locations. *Reveries of a Bachelor* – one of Emily Dickinson's favourite books – is a series of musings about life, marriage, dreams and travel.

This library is also heavy on adventure (*The Magnetic North* charts the search for a missing brother in Alaska), especially with a seafaring theme – Fenimore Cooper's *The Pilot* was responsible for unleashing a stream of maritime fiction. In terms of non-fiction, there is also plenty to digest, such as *My Apingi Kingdom*, a classic study of African wildlife, culture and tribes in the mid-1800s.

A HUMAN LIBRARY

Muslim

Refugee

Gay

Transgender

Dyslexic

Transsexual

Young Offender

Post-Traumatic Stress
  Disorder

Ex-Offender

Lesbian

Young Black Male

Wheelchair User

Jewish

Christian

Down Syndrome

Cerebral Palsy

Recovering Alcoholic

Teenage Mother

Schizophrenia

Bi-Polar

Ex-Substance Misuser

Unemployed

Autistic

Chav

HIV Positive

Learning Disability

Dyslexic

Borderline Personality
  Disorder

Bisexual

Homeless

Buddhist

Facial Disfigurement

Have you had a chat with any really good books recently? One that really broadened your horizons? If not, then keep an eye out for your nearest Human Library.

While traditional libraries are still essentially repositories of books, there are many kinds of modern ones from which you can borrow other items, such as toys, bicycles, tools, seeds and telescopes. At a Human Library event, the 'books' are people with special experiences – 'readers' can choose from various 'titles' (this list is the Human Library UK's suggestion of forty from which a dozen or so would make a good stock), and then 'borrow' them. They then 'read' the 'book' by (respectfully) asking the person questions about their personal situation.

According to the Human Library UK:

> The titles celebrate diversity and promote equality by deliberately acknowledging differences, lifestyles, ethnicities, faiths, disabilities, abilities and characteristics that may be stigmatised in the hope it might provoke an assumption or even prejudice in Readers. By then giving Readers the opportunity to borrow them for a safe and respectful conversation, the Human Library has the potential to challenge the prejudices, stereotypes and stigmas that can lead to discrimination.

The first event was held in 2000 in Copenhagen and since then the Human Library Organization, founded by Ronni Abergel, has become an international phenomenon with 'libraries' in more than seventy countries.

Each human book is a volunteer and, as well as answering pertinent questions, has the option not to answer and also to ask their own questions. What they are not supposed to do is turn the conversation into story-telling or self-promotion.

Human Libraries use familiar terminology. At the main desk there is a list of 'books' available and each Reader is given a Human Library card by one of the Librarians. They then choose a 'book' – sometimes with the help of an official Matchmaker or Library Assistant – and are introduced by a member of the library staff (while waiting to be chosen, the Books wait in a separate area called the Bookshelf and frequently borrow each other on an ad hoc basis). They then move to the Reading Room where there are numerous tables and chairs; this is where the conversation begins and lasts for up to half an hour.

As with all reading material, there are sometimes issues with the content. Plans for a Human Library event at Lenin Library in St Petersburg in 2016 were challenged when the host venue requested that four of the books scheduled to appear – the sex worker, the person without a child, the ex-prisoner and the homosexual – should be asked not to be present.

Human Library events are already held in schools, and a new pilot scheme is now being trialled in large companies along similar lines called 'Borrow a Co-worker'.

DAVID BYRNE'S PRIVATE LIBRARY: B

Brazilian Popular Music and Citizenship by Idelber Avelar and Christopher Dunn

Botsford Collection of Folk Songs Volumes 1 and 2 by Florence Hudson Botsford

Bourbon Street Black: The New Orleans Black Jazzman by Jack V. Buerkle and Danny Barker

Bicycle Diaries by David Byrne

Bossa Nova: The Story of the Brazilian Music that Seduced the World by Ruy Castro

Brutality Garden: Tropicalia and the Emergence of a Brazilian Counterculture by Christopher Dunn

But Beautiful: A Book About Jazz by Geoff Dyer

Black Rhythms of Peru: Reviving African Musical Heritage in the Black Pacific by Heidi Carolyn Feidman

Bound for Glory by Woody Guthrie

Blues Guitar: The Men Who Made the Music by Jas Obrecht

Bachata: A Social History of a Dominican Popular Music by
  Deborah Pacini Hernandez
Beats of the Heart: Popular Music of the World
The Man Who Fell To Earth by Jeremy Marre and Hannah
  Charlton
Bandalism: The Rock Group Survival Guide by Julian Ridgway
Black Music of Two Worlds by John Storm Roberts
Bug Music: How Insects Gave Us Rhythm and Noise by David
  Rothenberg

When musician David Byrne curated the 2015 Meltdown Festival at the Southbank Centre in London, he also included a surprise attraction – the chance to borrow books from his personal library of music books.

'I love a library,' he wrote in the *Guardian* newspaper, explaining that while he was growing up, the local library was virtually the only place where he could find out about the exciting things going on in the wider world.

The eclectic stock of 250 books shipped over from New York covered many musical subjects and continents, though Byrne admitted he had not read every one and that poetry was not a major part of his reading. The list above is just the ones beginning with B, though the whole library list has been put online by Maria Popova at her engaging *Brain Pickings* site via eagle-eyed reader Ben Hart.

Potential readers had to apply to obtain a special David Byrne Library card, but he was phlegmatic about people pinching one or two titles. Not all owners of private libraries have been so lucky. Noted book kleptomaniac Apellicon of Teos had his entire collection stolen by the Roman general Sulla in 84 BC, while Elizabethan polymath

John Dee found that when he returned from travelling around Europe in the 1580s, his brother-in-law Nicholas Fromond had, as he put it himself, 'unduely sold it presently upon my departure, or caused it to be carried away'. The Royal College of Physicians library holds more than 100 volumes stolen from Dee, including his copy of *The Prince* by Niccolo Machiavelli.

THE LIBRARY OF BABEL

Every book ever written

There are some quite exceptionally well-stocked reading rooms. In the Doctor Who episode 'Silence in the Library', the Doctor and his companion Donna travel to the 51st century and a library the size of a planet. Similarly, the Great Jedi Library (a.k.a. Library of Ossus) is a vast arrangement of buildings in *Star Wars*, though one with some notable similarities to the Long Room of Trinity College Library, Dublin.

The most famous 'one of everything' archive is Jorge Luis Borges' Library of Babel. This is a spectacularly huge, yet not quite infinite, series of adjoining hexagonal rooms lined with bookshelves which contain every book ever written and every permutation possible – each shelf has 35 books each exactly 410 pages long, every page has 40 lines and each line has 80 letters. The result is that, exactly like the internet, there are plenty of gems but these are overwhelmed by indecipherable gibberish, making the library barely usable.

Back in the real world, the Library of Alexandria was probably the nearest humankind has ever got to a library containing every book every written, and even then the most wildly exaggerated guesses suggest it could have contained only 70 per cent of everything in existence.

The obvious problems with such a massive accession programme have not stopped people trying to put together a modern Library of Babel. Programmer Jonathan Basile has put together an online version of the nearest anybody has got so far at libraryofbabel.info – you can search for any text, browse by hexagonal room and shelf, and simply pick something at random. In keeping with Borges' original concept, it is both all-encompassing and almost entirely unreadable.

Though Basile makes an excellent attempt on his site to explain how the library works and the computations involved, it can still be hard to fully grasp the size of the problem. Raymond Queneau's *Cent Mille Milliard des Poemes* (1961) helps put it in perspective. His small book contains ten sonnets, each with fourteen lines. The book is made up of strips so that you can flick backwards and forwards to make up your own sonnet. Even working steadily, reading a sonnet a minute for eight hours solid each day, it would take millions of years simply to read every variation of this one book.

Simply making a list of every book is a hugely daunting task. The ongoing and online Penguin Checklist Project, which aims to bring together in one place every book published by Penguin since 1935, shows that even attempting it for a single publisher is an enormous challenge. Going several steps further is The Open Library, part of the Internet Archive. Its goal is a searchable catalogue of details about every book in the world (it has already noted over 20 million books, though it only has one of the three I have written).

THE BOOKS ON THE INTERNATIONAL SPACE STATION

Canals in the Sand by Kevin J. Anderson
A Spell for Chameleon by Piers Anthony
The Source of Magic by Piers Anthony
Key to Havoc by Piers Anthony
The Moon's Shadow by Catherine Asaro
A Roll of the Dice by Catherine Asaro
Foundation and Empire by Isaac Asimov
Alien Infection by Darrell Bain
A Strange Valley by Darrell Bain
Darwin's Radio by Greg Bear
The Holy Road by Michael Blake
The Americans: The National Experience by Daniel J. Boorstin
The Americans: The Democratic Experience by Daniel J. Boorstin
The Americans: The Colonial Experience by Daniel J. Boorstin
Tanequil by Terry Brooks
The Wishsong of Shannara by Terry Brooks
Jarka Ruus: High Druid of Shannara by Terry Brooks
The Elfstones of Shannara by Terry Brooks
The Sword of Shannara by Terry Brooks
The Da Vinci Code by Dan Brown
Angels & Demons by Dan Brown
Bryson's Dictionary of Troublesome Words by Bill Bryson

Cetaganda by Lois McMaster Bujold

The Mountains of Mourning by Lois McMaster Bujold

Ethan of Athos by Lois McMaster Bujold

The Curse of Chalion by Lois McMaster Bujold

The Warrior's Apprentice by Lois McMaster Bujold

The Vor Game by Lois McMaster Bujold

Paladin of Souls by Lois McMaster Bujold

Falling Free by Lois McMaster Bujold

Brothers in Arms by Lois McMaster Bujold

Barrayar by Lois McMaster Bujold

The Spirit Ring by Lois McMaster Bujold

The Rule of Four by Ian Caldwell

Single & Single by John Le Carré

The Constant Gardener by John Le Carré

Absolute Friends by John Le Carré

1901 by Robert Conroy

The Last of the Mohicans by James Fenimore Cooper

State of Fear by Michael Crichton

The Universe at Midnight: Observations Illuminating the Cosmos
   by Ken Crosswell

On the Origin of Species by Charles Darwin

Collapse by Jared Diamond

A Tale of Two Cities by Charles Dickens

The Man who Killed his Brother by Stephen R. Donaldson

The Brothers Karamazov by Fyodor Dostoyevsky

Heroes of History by Will Durant

Arrows to the Moon by Chris Gainor

Faust by Johann Wolfgang von Goethe

Eyes of an Eagle: A Novel of Gravity Controlled by S.A. Gorden

Skipping Christmas by John Grisham

Systematic Theology by Wayne Grudem

The Federalist Papers (a collection of essays written in support
    of the Constitution of the United States by Alexander
    Hamilton, James Madison and John Jay)
Pandor's Star by Peter F. Hamilton
The Moon is a Harsh Mistress by Robert A. Heinlein
Catch As Catch Can: Collected Stories and Writings by
    Joseph Heller
Snow: The Prologue to Winter's Heart by Robert Jordan
Glimmers of the Pattern by Robert Jordan
Under the Banner of Heaven by Jon Krakauer
*Failure is Not an Option: Mission Control from Mercury to
    Apollo 13 and Beyond* by Gene Kranz
*Atom: An Odyssey from the Big Bang to Life on Earth and
    Beyond* by Lawrence M. Krauss
Who Moved My Rice? by Michael LaRocca
A Year with C.S. Lewis by C.S. Lewis
1776 by David McCullough
Gone with the Wind by Margaret Mitchell
*The Blue Sweater: Bridging the Gap Between Rich and Poor
    in an Interconnected World* by Jacqueline Novogratz
London Bridges by James Patterson
The Years of Rice and Salt by Kim Stanley Robinson
Dress Your Family in Corduroy and Denim by David Sedaris
Gone for Soldiers by Jeff Shaara
Ten Day MBA by Steven Silbiger
A Winter Haunting by Dan Simmons
Vanity Fair by William Makepeace Thackeray
War and Peace by Leo Tolstoy
Counting Up, Counting Down by Harry Turtledove
Mars Is No Place for Children by Mary E. Turzillo
Around the World in Eighty Days by Jules Verne

20,000 Leagues Under the Sea by Jules Verne
Lost Soldiers by James H. Webb
The Short Victorious War by David Weber
On Basilisk Station by David Weber
March to the Stars by David Weber
March to the Sea by David Weber
March Upcountry by David Weber
In Enemy Hands by David Weber
The Honor of the Queen by David Weber
Empire from the Ashes by David Weber
Echoes of Honor by David Weber
Crown of Slaves by David Weber
Ashes of Victory by David Weber
Honor Among Enemies by David Weber
The Apocalypse Troll by David Weber
Birmingham Then and Now by J.D. Weeks
Witness Walter by Jon Williams
The Jeeves Omnibus by P.G. Wodehouse
The Schopenhauer Cure by Irvin D. Yalom
Creating a World Without Poverty by Muhammad Yunus
Russian–English Dictionary
Oxford Dictionary of World History
Oxford Dictionary of Philosophy
Asimov's Science Fiction (five copies)
Analog Science Fiction and Fact (various issues)

CHILDREN'S BOOKS:
Rosie Revere, Engineer by Andrea Beaty
The Incredible Intergalactic Journey Home
Max Goes to Jupiter: A Science Adventure by Jeffrey Bennett
Max Goes to the International Space Station by Jeffrey Bennett

The Wizard Who Saved the World by Jeffrey Bennett
Max Goes to Mars by Jeffrey Bennett
I, Humanity by Jeffrey Bennett
The Rhino Who Swallowed a Storm by LeVar Burton and Susan
　Schaefer Bernado
Mousetronaut by Mark Kelly
Endeavour's Long Journey by John Danny Olivas

The astronauts on the International Space Station are obviously busy people, but even busy people need some time to relax and unwind. In addition to a well-stocked film library (particularly strong on movies with a space theme, including 2001: *A Space Odyssey* and *Gravity*), there are also plenty of books in their informal library.

Some are brought up by the astronauts – Susan Helms was allowed ten paperbacks and chose *Gone With the Wind*, *Vanity Fair* and *War and Peace* in her carry-on. Others come with space tourists such as billionaire businessman Charles Simonyi, who brought *Faust* and Robert Heinlein's *The Moon is a Harsh Mistress*.

There is also an excellent ongoing project called 'Story Time from Space' that encourages children's interest in reading and space by sending selected titles to the ISS. Video recordings of the astronauts (including Tim Peake) reading them aloud are then published online.

LYDIA LANGUISH'S CIRCULATING
LIBRARY SELECTION

The Memoirs of Lady Woodford (Anonymous)

The Memoirs of a Lady of Quality, Written by Herself
   (Anonymous)

The Whole Duty of Man (Anonymous)

The Tears of Sensibility by François-Thomas-Marie de Baculard
   d'Arnaud (translated by John Murdoch)

Mrs. Chapone [*Letters on the Improvement of the Mind
   Addressed to a Young Lady* by Hester Chapone]

Lord Chesterfield's Letters

The Fatal Connexion by Mrs Fogerty

Fordyce's Sermons [*Sermons to Young Women* by James
   Fordyce]

The Delicate Distress by Elizabeth Griffith

The Gordian Knot by Richard Griffith

The Man of Feeling by Henry Mackenzie

Ovid (various works)

The Innocent Adultery by Paul Scarron (an English translation
   of *L'Adultere Innocente*)

Peregrine Pickle by Tobias Smollett

Humphry Clinker by Tobias Smollett

Roderick Random by Tobias Smollett

The Sentimental Journey (second volume) by Laurence Sterne

The Mistakes of the Heart by Pierre Henri Treyssac de Vergy

The Reward of Constancy (unknown author)

Lord Aimworth [*The History of Lord Aimworth, and the
   Honourable Charles Hartford, Esq. in a series of letters, a
   novel, by the author of Dorinda Catsby and Ermina, or the
   Fair Recluse*] (unknown author)

'Madam, a circulating library in a town is as an evergreen tree of diabolical knowledge'
Sir Anthony Absolute, The Rivals

In Richard Brinsley Sheridan's classic 18th-century comedy of manners The Rivals, Lydia Languish's taste for romantic fiction is revealed in several key scenes, chiefly in the list of books that she asks her maid Lucy to borrow from a circulating library in Bath (the actual names of the works mentioned in the play are given in [square brackets]).

There are one or two titles among the twenty books mentioned which are familiar to 21st-century readers, but most have largely fallen by the wayside. Indeed, there is even some debate about which book is referred to as The Reward of Constancy – perhaps The Happy Pair or, Virtue and Constancy Rewarded by a Mr Shebbeare, or maybe more likely the anonymously authored Belinda; or, Happiness the Reward of Constancy, Mannifested in a Series of the Most Interesting and Surprising Events Ever Yet Made Publick.

Some of the titles did not receive a positive press at the time. 'Romantic nonsense' was The London Magazine's summing up in 1773 of The Fatal Connexion by Mrs Fogerty, one of the popular sentimental works at which Sheridan was poking fun. Others, though, were extremely popular. The anonymously-written Whole Duty of Man, a Protestant devotional, was a 'must have' title in respectable homes and mentioned in Thomas Hardy's The Mayor of Casterbridge as being a frequent shelf-fellow to the Bible and the works of biblical chronicler Josephus.

The Delicate Distress – a copy of which Lucy decides not to buy because Lady Slattern Lounger 'had so soiled and dog's-eared it, it wa'n't fit for a Christian to read' – was Elizabeth Griffith's most popular fiction and written from a resolutely feminist perspective. It consists of a series of intelligent letters written between two sisters about how to live an ethical life. It was published in conjunction with her husband Richard's *The Gordian Knot*, a rare domestic literary double-act.

Along similar lines was another of the many popular books on conduct of the period, *Letters on the Improvement of the Mind Addressed to a Young Lady* by Hester Chapone. These pieces of advice to her teenage niece about the importance of rational thought achieved through reading and study – but specifically not through sentimental fiction, such as Mackenzie's *The Man of Feeling* – quickly went through multiple editions and foreign translations.

It was cited by Mary Wollstonecraft as an almost unique example of a genuinely useful self-improvement book and influenced her famous *A Vindication of the Rights of Woman*. The other point of view is argued in James Fordyce's *Sermons to Young Women*, which argues that women need to be meek and modest, yet still dress well and make themselves beautiful. This was also hugely popular – Mr Collins reads part of it to the Bennets in *Pride and Prejudice*, somewhat to Lydia's horror – and was also savaged by Wollstonecraft.

A TELEPHONE BOX LIBRARY

The Dying Hours by Mark Billingham
The Cruellest Game by Hilary Bonner
Night of the Wolf by Alice Borchardt

The Chosen One by Sam Bourne
The Well by Catherine Chanter
A Wanted Man by Lee Child
Red Bones by Ann Cleeves
Step By Step Low Fat Cookbook by Rosemary Conley
Jump! by Jilly Cooper
Very Rude Limericks by Stephen Cordwell
Living a Lie by Josephine Cox
Valhalla Rising by Clive Cussler
Thanks for Nothing by Jack Dee
Hens Reunited by Lucy Diamond
The Year of Taking Chances by Lucy Diamond
The Secrets of Happiness by Lucy Diamond
Me and Mr Jones by Lucy Diamond
The Excalibur Codex by James Douglas
In Stitches: The Highs and Lows of Life as an A&E Doctor by
    Nick Edwards
Love Always by Harriet Evans
The Mask of Troy by David Gibbons
Cut by Cathy Glass
V is for Vengeance by Sue Grafton
The 125 Best Recipes Ever by Loyd Grossman
When the Lights Go On Again by Annie Groves
Lights of Liverpool by Ruth Hamilton
The Summer Guest by Emma Hannigan
The Complete Practical Encyclopedia of Running by Elizabeth
    Hufton
Winter Games by Rachel Johnson
Good Behaviour by Molly Keane
A Girl's Best Friend by Lindsey Kelk
Survival of the Fittest by Jonathan Kellerman

The Final Minute by Simon Kernick
Shopaholic to the Rescue by Sophie Kinsella
A Conspiracy of Paper by David Liss
My Autobiography by A.P. McCoy
When Daddy Comes Home by Toni Maguire
Eclipse by Stephanie Meyer
The Stranger Inside by Shannon Moroney
The Secret Life of a Slummy Mummy by Fiona Neill
An Inspector Calls by J.B. Priestley
Gordon Ramsay's Secrets
Gordan Ramsay's Healthy Appetite
The Almost Moon by Alice Sebold
Throne of the Caesars by Harry Sidebottom
Through it All I've Always Laughed: Memoirs of Count Arthur Strong
Fear of the Collar by Patrick Touher
The Secret Life of France by Lucy Wadham
Equinox by Michael White
The Shadow of the Wind by Carlos Ruiz Zafon

Libraries are at risk wherever you look, but there is one growth area amid the swirl of cutbacks and closures. By the end of the 20th century, British Telecom had erected more than 90,000 of its iconic red phone boxes designed by Giles Gilbert Scott around Britain. Now, around half of them have been removed, but instead of simply demolishing the rest, many local communities have taken them over and are running them as useful civic spaces. One of the most popular repurposings has been as a neighbourhood library.

Local residents borrow and return books from the newly built shelves inside on an honesty basis, adding their own

books to the shelves to swell numbers. These libraries'
stock is constantly changing, but this list is a snapshot of
the stock at Knightshayes in Devon in late summer 2016,
courtesy of writer and journalist Emma Townshend.

A cousin of the telephone box library concept is the
Little Free Library project. These are small, bird-box-like
libraries which have been set up in mainly residential
neighbourhoods in front gardens and yards, largely in the
USA but also around the world. Again, there are no library
cards and no fines – anybody can, as the LFL's motto has
it, 'Take a book, return a book'. There are now 50,000 in
operation.

MASS OBSERVATION (1): LUCCOMBE'S TYPICAL BOOKCASES

Daisy's Aunt by E.F. Benson
The Light of Scarthey by Egerton Castle
The Top of the World by E.M. Dell
The Soul of Gold by Justus Miles Forman
The Little Man by John Galsworthy
The Case of the Howling Dog by E.S. Gardner
Trooper O'Neil by George Goodchild
Cleopatra by H. Rider Haggard
A Modern Circe by Margaret Wolfe Hungerford
Molly Bawn by Margaret Wolfe Hungerford
Britain under Shellfire by F. Illingworth
True Blue by W.H.G. Kingston
Idols by W.J. Locke
White Fang by Jack London

Sister Teresa by George Moore
John of Gerisan by John Oxenham
Enquire Within Upon Everything edited by Robert Kemp Philp
My Official Wife by R.H. Savage
The Danger Line by Joan Sutherland
Two bibles
Two prayer books
The Great Book of Humour
Two or three *Lilliputs*, *Home Notes* and *Life*
Webster's Improved English Dictionary
Minehead: A Guidebook
The Woman's Weekly Bedside Book

Established in 1937, the Mass Observation project aimed to document the daily lives of the working class in Britain and consequently give them a non-stereotyped voice. Hundreds of volunteers, and some paid investigators, interviewed and photographed people around the nation about a huge range of subjects.

During the Second World War, the organisation started to work more closely with the government and in 1947 began publishing a series of books called *British Ways of Life*. *Exmoor Village* by W.J. Turner, with colour photographs by John Hinde, was the first (the second, and as it turned out last, was *British Circus Life*) and turned the magnifying glass on the Somerset village of Luccombe. Mr Turner described it as 'an authentic account of the way of life, the outlook, and feelings of the people described'.

As well as interviews with villagers and their thoughts on pets, politics and education, there were marvellous charts designed by the Isotype Institute, and an appendix listing the contents of a typical Luccombe bookcase (previous page). The book – not entirely welcomed by the residents, some of whom felt their privacy had been invaded – was part of a general commerical effort to celebrate traditional rural England and use that image to encourage foreign investment.

Among the interesting titles in the typical bookcase is the marvellously titled Enquire Within Upon Everything. Subtitled 'A Comprehensive Guide to the Necessities of Domestic Life in Victorian Britain', it covered everything from how to tell if food is fresh and etiquette tips to employment law, how to model a flower in wax, and cures for baldness. It went into more than 100 editions and sold over 1.5 million copies. Inspired by the book, Tim Berners-Lee used the name ENQUIRE for his initial version of the World Wide Web. Other items of interest include Molly Bawn, which contains the first usage of the phrase 'Beauty is in the eye of the beholder', and My Official Wife, an adventure story involving Russian Nihilists and international assassination attempts.

The appendix includes a second 'typical bookcase' which includes more religious titles as well as Gulliver's Travels by Jonathan Swift, 'four very old paperback novels', six volumes of The Gardener's Assistant, and three cookery books issued by Arnold's Self-raising Flour.

MPS' MOST-BORROWED BOOKS

How Parliament Works by Robert Rogers and Rhodri Walters
Why the Tories Won: The Inside Story of the 2015 Election by
    Tim Ross

Speaking Out: Lessons in Life and Politics by Ed Balls
*Coalition: The Inside Story of the Conservative–Liberal
    Democrats Coalition Government* by David Laws
*The Second Machine Age: Work, Progress and Prosperity in
    a Time of Brilliant Technologies* by Erik Brynjolfsson and
    Andrew McAfee
Parliament Ltd: A Journey to the Dark Heart of British Politics
    by Martin Williams
Can the Welfare State Survive? by Andrew Gamble
Capital in the Twenty-First Century by Thomas Piketty
This is London by Ben Judah
Politics: Between the Extremes by Nick Clegg
Joseph Chamberlain: A Most Radical Imperialist by Travis
    L. Crosby
How to be a Parliamentary Researcher by Robert Dale
How to be a Government Whip by Helen Jones
Why Nations Fail: The Origins of Power, Prosperity, and Poverty
    by Daron Acemoglu and James A. Robinson
Them and Us: Changing Britain – Why We Need a Fair Society
    by Will Hutton
Student Power! The Radical Days of the English Universities by
    Esmee Sinead Hanna
*The Spirit Level: Why More Equal Societies Almost Always Do
    Better* by Richard Wilkinson and Kate Pickett
*The Rise of the Robots: Technology and the Threat of Mass
    Unemployment* by Martin Ford
Parliament: The Biography. Vol. 1: Ancestral Voices by Chris Bryant

Each year, the House of Commons Library puts together
a list of its most-borrowed books by MPs and their staff.
The most recent one, in descending order of number of

withdrawals, is topped (as it has been most years since 2008) by the useful self-help guide *How Parliament Works*.

Another regular popular choice – though less so in the last couple of years – has been Paul Flynn's step-by-step guide to being a successful MP. As Brandon Robshaw, reviewing the book in the *Independent*, puts it, 'This wry, sardonic account reveals that MPs must have the most arcane, illogical, inefficient, unreasonable and capricious set of rules governing their working lives of any job in the world.'

Understandably, the borrowings list over the years is dominated by serious political and economic titles, plus a good spread of political biographies (Alan Johnson's autobiographies often appear and *Roy Jenkins: A Well-Rounded Life* by John Campbell topped the list in 2014).

The only other entries have been:

Culture and the Death of God by Terry Eagleton (sixth most borrowed) in 2015

Rough Guide to Berlin by John Gawthrop (third) in 2014

Alex Ferguson: My Autobiography (equal fourth) in 2014

Mindful Manifesto: How Doing Less and Noticing More Can Help us Thrive in a Stressed-out World by Jonty Heaversedge (equal sixth) in 2013

Lonely Planet: Myanmar by John Allen (equal sixth) in 2013

Feral: Searching for Enchantment on the Frontiers of Rewilding by George Monbiot (seventh in 2013)

There is a lighter side to MPs' reading, though, as revealed in a poll by Blackwells in 2016 of the members' summer reading intentions. Topped by Boris Johnson's biography of Winston Churchill, *The Churchill Factor*, the list was full of titles about the Second World War and America, but there was also room in the suitcases for the following novels and poetry:

The Night Manager by John Le Carré
I Am Pilgrim by Terry Hayes
The Poisonwood Bible by Barbara Kingsolver
The Art of Falling by Kim Moore
The Wolf Trial by Neil Mackay
The Immigration Handbook by Caroline Smith
A Spool of Blue Thread by Anne Tyler
Grandpa's Great Escape by David Walliams

QUEEN MARY'S DOLL'S HOUSE LIBRARY

Vespers by A.A. Milne
Autobiography of J.M. Barrie
Meditations of a Refugee by Sir Max Beerbohm
Songs of Innocence by William Blake
Peter and Paul by Hilaire Belloc
Christmas Eve and New Year's Eve by Arnold Bennett
The Battle of the Somme by John Buchan
The Nursery of the Craft: From The Mirror of the Sea by
    Joseph Conrad
The Broad Highway: A Romance of Kent by Jeffrey Farnol
Poems: Abridged for Dolls and Princes by Robert Graves
Poems by Aldous Huxley
The Doll's-house Cookery Book by Agnes Jekyll
The Garden by Gertrude Jekyll

Verses by Rudyard Kipling
The Princess and the Nightingale by William Somerset Maugham
The Garden of Contentment by Elinor Mordaunt
Star Dust, or Verses from Sappho by Sappho
R.L.S. in a Nutshell by Robert Louis Stevenson
Principles of Doll-surgery by Sir John Bland-Sutton

Designed and built in the early 1920s by Sir Edward Lutyens for the wife of George V, Queen Mary's Doll's House is an impressive 1:12 scale miniature town house, with flushing lavatories, sprung beds, hot and cold running water, and a garden designed by Gertrude Jekyll. It also contains an atmospheric walnut-panelled working library.

Lutyens asked many famous writers to contribute to the library, which features around 200 postage-stamp-sized volumes, an abridged catalogue of which is listed above. Other authors who took part include Edith Wharton, Thomas Hardy and H. Rider Haggard. Most are in manuscript but a few are printed. The Queen's daughter Princess Marie Louise personally wrote to each of the writers asking for either an original composition or a suitable passage from work already published. Those who agreed – George Bernard Shaw and Virginia Woolf declined the offer – were sent blank volumes to write in and return. The results were bound in vellum or Morocco leather, the majority by Sangorski & Sutcliffe, and each has a bookplate designed by E.H. Shepard.

Most of the books are original works which were written specifically for the doll's house, such as Max Beerbohm's *Meditations of a Refugee*, Anthony Hope's *A Tragedy in Outline* and M.R. James's *The Haunted Dolls' House*. Kipling added some unpublished poems to his selection as well as some of his own illustrations. There are also four tiny Bibles, a Koran, a complete Shakespeare, two stamp albums (in attractive slipcases), a stocklist of wines and spirits in the doll's house cellars, and an atlas with numerous maps of the world (British possessions naturally shown in red). The copy of *Carmina Sapphica* by Horace was provided by the famous Ashendene Press. It was part of a very small run of about ten, all bound in red Niger. Less than half of these are now thought to exist.

Two of the books have since been published as exact reproductions of the miniature originals. In 'How Watson Learned the Trick' by Sir Arthur Conan Doyle, the great detective's assistant tries to show Sherlock Holmes that that 'there are other people in the world who can be as clever as you' when it comes to deduction. However, Holmes shows him it is not that easy. In 'J. Smith' by Cyril Kenneth Bird, better known as the cartoonist Fougasse, a fairy is blown out of fairyland by a strong wind into Eaton Square, and has several adventures in 1920s London.

SCOTTISH PRISONERS' FAVOURITE BOOKS

1. *The Book of Glasgow Murders* by Donald M. Fraser
2. *The Resurrection of Johnny Cash: Hurt, Redemption, and American Recordings* by Graeme Thompson
3. *Tough Talk* by Arthur White and Ian McDowall
4. *NYPD Red* by James Patterson
5. *Game of Thrones* by George R.R. Martin
6. *Gone* by Michael Grant

7. *City of Gangs: Glasgow and the Rise of the British Gangster*
   by Andrew Davies
8. *Revenge* by Martina Cole
9. *Greed* by Chris Ryan
10. *The Hunger Games* by Suzanne Collins

The Scottish Prison Service released the full list of books available to inmates in Scotland for the first time in 2015, as well as information about the most-borrowed books by prisoners. At HMP Edinburgh, Irvine Welsh was the most popular author, while the *Driving Theory Test For Cars* topped the list in Perth. Above are the top ten books at Barlinnie and below the top ten from HMP Grampian's library:

1. *Animal Farm* by George Orwell
2. *Heroes and Villains: The Good, The Mad, The Bad and The Ugly* by Charles Bronson
3. *Honour Among Thieves* by Jeffrey Archer
4. *The Catcher in the Rye* by J.D. Salinger
5. *Two Women* by Martina Cole
6. *The Body Art Book* by Jean-Chris Miller
7. *100 Tips for Acoustic Guitar* by David Mead
8. *Chocolate Cakes for Weddings and Celebrations* by John Slattery
9. *The Art of Walt Disney* by Christopher Finch
10. *Labyrinth* by Randall Sullivan

The Books in the Nick scheme provides books to prisoners who are only in police custody. Established by Metropolitan police special constable Steve Whitmore, it makes available a range of poetry, short stories and graphic novels in English and various foreign languages, as well as classics such as *The Catcher in the Rye* by J.D. Salinger, *To Kill a Mockingbird* by Harper Lee and *Animal Farm* by George Orwell.

The importance of reading to prison life is also a constant element in the popular television series *Orange is the New Black*, in which the inmates constantly have books on the go. Many dramatic scenes even take place in the prison library. Below is a selection of those read in Season 4:

Americanah by Chimamanda Ngozi Adichie
How to Stop Worrying and Start Living by Dale Carnegie
Dhalgren by Samuel R. Delany
Lord of the Flies by William Golding
Bird by Bird by Anne Lamott
Pêcheur d'Islande by Pierre Loti
The Longest Way Home by Andrew McCarthy
The Wise Man's Fear by Patrick Rothfuss
The Forgotten Affairs of Youth by Alexander McCall Smith
What Makes Sammy Run? by Budd Schulberg

MARILYN MONROE'S PRIVATE LIBRARY

16 Famous European Plays, compiled by Bennett Cerf and Van H. Cartmell
Theatre '52 by John Chapman
Thirteen by Corwin, by Norman Corwin
More by Corwin, by Norman Corwin
Untitled & Other Radio Dramas by Norman Corwin
Critics' Choice by Jack Gaver
The Potting Shed by Graham Greene

Modern American Dramas by Harlan Hatcher
The Complete Plays of Henry James
Born Yesterday by Garson Kanin
Politics in the American Drama by Caspar Nannes
Long Day's Journey Into Night by Eugene O'Neill (two copies)
Elizabethan Plays edited by Hazelton Spencer
Sons of Men by Herschel Steinhardt
Best American Plays: Third Series, 1945–1951
The Album of the Cambridge Garrick Club

Although Marilyn Monroe is best known for her roles in films such as Some Like It Hot and The Seven Year Itch, she was also a keen reader.

The list of plays above were all part of her personal library, auctioned off by Christies in New York in 1999. Impressive work by her aficionados at the online fan site Everlasting Star has added many more titles to her known collection – a total of around 400 titles – through published interviews or photographs. It is an eclectic mix, ranging from Thurber Country by James Thurber and The Great Gatsby by F. Scott Fitzgerald, to God Protect Me From My Friends by Gavin Maxwell and plays by Aristophanes. There was also space on her shelves for Pet Turtles by Julien Bronson, Justine by Lawrence Durrell (two copies), and Das Kapital by Karl Marx. Among her first editions was On the Road by Jack Kerouac.

One of the most famous photos of Marilyn Monroe reading a book, in this case James Joyce's Ulysses, was taken in a children's playground in Long Island by Eve Arnold for Esquire magazine in 1955. Arnold says that Marilyn admitted finding it a difficult read, but was enjoying it nevertheless.

Chapter Four
JUNIOR CHOICE

THE BOOKS ALAN TURING BORROWED
FROM HIS SCHOOL LIBRARY

Isotopes by William Frederick Aston

Mathematical Recreations and Essays by W.W. Rouse Ball

Alice's Adventures in Wonderland by Lewis Carroll

The Game of Logic by Lewis Carroll

Through the Looking Glass by Lewis Carroll

The Common Sense of the Exact Sciences by William Kingdon
Clifford

Space, Time and Gravitation by Sir Arthur Stanley Eddington

The Nature of the Physical World by Sir Arthur Stanley
Eddington

Sidelights on Relativity by Albert Einstein

The Escaping Club by A.J. Evans

Contributions to Mental Philosophy by Immanuel Hermann
Fichte (translated and edited by J.D. Morell)

The New Physics by Arthur Haas (translated by R.W. Lawson)

Supply and Demand by Hubert D. Henderson

The Stars in their Courses by Sir James Hopwood Jeans

The Universe Around Us by Sir James Hopwood Jeans

Atoms and Rays by Sir Oliver Lodge

Phases of Modern Science by Sir Oliver Lodge et al.

Matter and Motion by James Clerk Maxwell

The Theory of Heat by Thomas Preston

A Selection of Photographs of Stars, Star-Clusters & Nebulae, together with information concerning the instruments & the methods employed in the pursuit of celestial photography by Isaac Roberts

Modern Chromatics: With Applications to Art and Industry by Ogden Nicholas Rood

A Short History of Mathematics by Vera Sanford

Celestial Objects for Common Telescopes by Thomas William Webb

The Recent Development of Physical Science by William Cecil Dampier Whetham

Science and the Modern World by Alfred North Whitehead

Sound Waves and their Uses by Alexander Wood

Journal of the Chemical Society, vols 95, 96, 97

Illusions (Anonymous)

Lead (Anonymous)

Modern Electric Theory (Anonymous)

Money (Anonymous)

Between 10 October 1928 and 16 May 1931, Alan Turing made good use of his school library. The list of what he checked out as a sixth former, put together by Sherborne School Library archivist Rachel Hassall and publicised by the popular mathematics author Alex Bellos, not altogether unsurprisingly shows that the future computer scientist and wartime code breaker read very widely in sciences.

Key texts include Einstein's *Sidelights on Relativity*, published in 1922, which is based on a series of his lectures and includes 'Ether and the Theory of Relativity', and 'Geometry and Experience', focusing on the concept of infinity. There is also Whitehead's seminal *Science and the Modern World* (a broader look at science in terms of culture and how it can be harnessed for social progress) and Jeans's science populariser *The Universe Around Us* (aimed at making the structure of the universe 'intelligible to readers with no special scientific knowledge').

The only lighter picks are the Lewis Carrolls, the Rouse Ball (and even that is fairly tough, with chapters on 'Medieval Problems' and 'The Kepler–Poinsot polyhedra') and the A.J. Evans adventure memoir, which details the author's daring escape from the 'escape-proof' Fort 9, the Colditz-like First World War camp in Ingolstadt.

Library records can certainly offer insights into the reading patterns and thoughts of historical figures. The New York Society Library holds details of all the founding fathers' borrowing histories, showing, for example, that George Washington took out Emer de Vattel's *The Law of Nations* on 5 October 1789, as well as Volume 12 of the *History of the Proceedings and Debates of the House of Commons*. In the following century, the library's records show Herman Melville borrowing William Scoresby's *Account of the Arctic Regions* and *Journal of the Northern Whale Fishery* on 13 June 1851 at the time he was finishing *Moby-Dick*. The library also holds some of the books they used – not copies, the actual ones they studied.

Sometimes library slips also come up for auction. This is how we know that J.D. Salinger took out *Death Took a Publisher* by Norman Forrest in December 1959 (it was due back on Christmas Eve but he brought it back two days early), and that thirteen-year-old Elvis Presley borrowed *The Courageous Heart: A Life of Andrew Jackson For Young Readers* by Bessi Rowland James and Marquis James from his high school library in 1948.

Should these library withdrawals be made public? Many librarians believe this kind of public release breaks an ethical code, as witnessed by the media horror when a Japanese newspaper revealed that as a schoolboy Haruki Murakami took out the three-volume complete works of French writer Joseph Kessel, author of *Belle de Jour*. Indeed, the FBI secretly targeted libraries as part of their counterintelligence work in the 1980s until their efforts were made public, and did so again after 9/11 until the American Library Assocation objected and managed to safeguard readers' privacy.

MASS OBSERVATION (2): BOOKS BORROWED BY CHILDREN VISITING LIBRARIES IN FULHAM IN MAY 1940

GIRLS:

Fire on the Seven Peaks by Ralph Arnold

Cat's Cradle for His Majesty by Margaret Baker[1]

Once Upon a Time: A Book of Old Time Fairy Tales by Katharine Lee Bates

Tales and Legends from India by M. Dorothy Belgrave and Hilda Hart

Harum Scarum Jill by Frederica Bennett

Young Yap by Olwen Bowen

The Secret of the Desert by Coutts Brisbane[2]

More of Milly-Molly-Mandy by Joyce Lankester Brisley
Captain of Springdale by Dorita Fairlie Bruce[3]
In Teddy Bear's House by Mrs H.C. Cradock
William the Detective by Richmal Crompton
William the Outlaw by Richmal Crompton
The New Girl at Greychurch by Winifred Darch[4]
Marathi Folk Tales by Wilfrid E. Dexter
The Adventures of Sherlock Holmes by Arthur Conan Doyle
The Chalet Girls in Camp by Elinor Brent-Dyer
The Rivals of the Chalet School by Elinor Brent-Dyer
The Doll's House by J.A. Grant
The Girls of Redlands by Pamela Tynan Hinkson
Mopsa the Fairy by Jean Ingelow[5]
John and Mary Abroad by Grace James[6]
John and Mary's Secret Society by Grace James
The Long Journey by Johannes V. Jensen[7]
The Raid by Captain W.E. Johns
Snipp, Snapp, Snurr and the Magic Horse by Maj Lindman[8]
The House at Pooh Corner by A.A. Milne
Magic for Marigold by Lucy Maud Montgomery
The Abbey Girls in Town by Elsie J. Oxenham[9]
Get-a-Way and Hary Janos by Maud and Miska Petersham[10]
Book of Goblins by William Heath Robinson
Fuzzy Peg the Hedgehog by Alison Uttley
John Wentley Takes Charge by John F.C. Westerman[11]
The Adventures of Mr Goodenough by Susan Mary Williams
Relief's Knocker by (?)
Our Eurpina's Story by (?)

BOYS:
Head of the School by Harold Avery
Babar at Home by Jean De Brunhoff
Boys' Book of Model Aeroplanes by Francis A. Collins
William the Good by Richmal Crompton
William's Crowded Hours by Richmal Crompton
William and the A.R.P. by Richmal Crompton
The Memoirs of Sherlock Holmes by Arthur Conan Doyle
Arnold Adair with the French Aces by Laurence La Tourette
  Driggs[12]
The Last War Trail by Edward S. Ellis[13]
The Hunted Piccaninnies by William Montgomerie Fleming
*Our Own Affairs, a Guide to the Intelligent Reading of the
  Newspaper* by Kathleen Gibberd
Parry Wins Through by R.A.H. Goodyear
She by H. Rider Haggard
I Find Australia by William Hatfield[14]
Sky Riders: A Book of Famous Flyers by Harry Harper
Dingy and Pips in Trouble by Anton Lind[15]
The Tale of Squirrel Nutkin by Beatrix Potter
The Tale of Mrs Tiggy Winkle by Beatrix Potter
The Scar on the Film by Wilfrid Robertson[16]
Heidi Grows Up by Charles Tritten[17]
The Tiger's Cub at School by Rowland Walker
Winkles, Schoolboy Detective by Rowland Walker
Lost City of Light by Capt. F.A.M. Webster[18]
The Air Record Breakers by J.F.C. Westerman
The Last of the Buccaneers by Percy F. Westerman[19]
The Sea Secrets of the Kestrel by (?)
Railways by (?)
52 Tales of Wildlife and Adventure by (?)

This is another book list put together by the Mass Observation researchers. It is divided between what girls and boys chose at the library; there is a heavy emphasis on school stories and an interestingly broad choice in both groups.

Notes

1 The story of a lucky cat told in silhouettes.

2 An adventure story in which Japan tries to invade Australia.

3 Bruce's girls' school stories were second only in popularity to Angela Brazil's. Her six Springdale books are set in a Scottish school.

4 Darch focused on girls' state school stories and on female teachers as well as pupils. Her books were popular with adults as well as children and teenagers.

5 A boy finds a nest of fairies and travels to Fairyland on the back of an albatross.

6 The John and Mary series is set in Berkshire and follows two bilingual Italian–English children living with their grandmother (and apparently never growing up) between the 1930s and 1960s.

7 *The Long Journey* (*Den Lange Rejse* in Danish) consists of six novels by the Danish winner of the Nobel Prize in Literature, Johannes V. Jensen. The main theme is evolution, and the books move from a pre-Ice Age setting up to Columbus's landing in America.

8 One in a series featuring fictional boy triplets from Sweden who have gentle adventures. A follow-up series featured the girl triplets Flicka, Ricka and Dicka.

9 There are thirty-eight titles in the Abbey Series of novels set in a girls' school. The last one sees the children of the

main characters start at their mothers' alma mater. Folk dancing and May Queens are recurrent themes throughout the series.

10 Two broken toys (Hary, a Hungarian soldier doll, and Get-A-Way, a stuffed horse) join forces and head for a promised land where old toys can become new.

11 John Francis Cyril Westerman was the son of Percy F. Westerman (see below). Most of his books for boys were about flying. His best-known character was the Biggles-lite hero Wentley, who initially works as a mail-delivery pilot but ends up as an independent aeroplane consultant.

12 Arnold Adair is a dashing American pilot created by Driggs, who was a tireless campaigner and populariser of the benefits of aviation in many areas, from the military to commercial fishing.

13 Edward Sylvester Ellis was a teacher and writer remembered largely for his trilogy of Deerfoot novels set at the end of the 18th century in Missouri, of which *The Last War* is the concluding title.

14 William Hatfield was a bushman in Australia who was especially interested in Aboriginal culture.

15 Anton Lind was an anonymous ghostwriter whose early fiction focused on the Foreign Legion, but he also wrote books set in boys' schools – Dingy and Pips are among the students at the fictional Altonbury.

16 A 'lost race' novel featuring an ancient Phoenician civilisation in Africa.

17 Based on the famous character created by Johanna Spyri. Here Heidi is away at a fancy boarding school but dreaming of her mountains ...

18 Captain F.A.M. Webster has been described as 'the father of

British athletics coaching'. He also wrote children's science and fantasy fiction, often with a 'lost race' theme (ancient Toltecs in Brazil, civilisations inside extinct volcanoes, Viking Amazons in Africa). *Lost City of Light* is a quest story in which a descendant of the Templars searches for a lost Christian city in Tibet and stumbles upon a dystopian Chinese city.

19 Percy Westerman's fiction for boys – he wrote more than 170 titles – has sold millions of copies. He lived and wrote on a converted Thames barge in Dorset.

THOM GUNN'S POETRY RECOMMENDATIONS FOR CHILDREN

The Poet's Tongue edited by W.H. Auden and John Garrett
The Beatles Song Book
The Bob Dylan Song Book
Howl and Other Poems and *Planet News* by Allen Ginsberg
Lupercal or Selected Poems by Ted Hughes
Selected Poems by D.H. Lawrence
Collected Poems by Wilfred Owen
Ariel by Sylvia Plath
Selected Poems by Ezra Pound
The Back Country by Gary Snyder

When Thom Gunn was asked by the Academy of American Poets to suggest which books he thought would be most engaging for English students at high school, he came up with a list of which the Nobel Prize in Literature awards committee would have approved.

'The first aim of someone teaching poetry in a high

school should be to continuously demonstrate that poetry is of many sorts and is all around us,' he replied, 'that a rhymed political slogan is poetry of a kind, for example, and the lyrics of a song by the Beatles, the Rolling Stones or Bob Dylan may be poetry of a very high order.' His letter especially picks out 'Eleanor Rigby' and Pound's 'The Ballad of the Goodly Fere'.

Gunn emphasises that Snyder and Ginsberg are particularly good at speaking to teenagers. 'True, there are references to sex and drugs,' he wrote, 'and I don't know what school policies may be about these. I think poems about sex and drugs are particularly good for teenagers to read.'

Poetry also features on Leo Tolstoy's list of the books he felt had the greatest effect on his life. In a letter to a friend, he divides up his reading life into five sections, so that from childhood to age fourteen he was especially impressed by (in his original order):

Tales from The Thousand and One Nights
'Napoleon' (poem) by Alexander Pushkin
The Little Black Hen by Antony Pogorelsky
The story of Joseph from the Bible
The Byliny (folk tales)

And from fourteen to twenty by:

The Conquest of Mexico by William Prescott
Tales of Good and Evil by Nikolai Gogol
Dead Souls by Nikolai Gogol
A Sentimental Journey by Laurence Sterne
A Hero for Our Time by Mikhail Lermontov

The Hapless Anton by Dmitry Grigorovich
Polinka Saks by Aleksandr Druzhinin
A Sportsman's Notebook by Ivan Turgenev
Die Räuber by Friedrich Schiller
Yevgeny Onegin by Alexander Pushkin
The Gospel of Matthew
The Confessions by Jean Jacques-Rousseau
Emile: Or An Education by Jean Jacques-Rousseau
'Viy' from *The Collected Tales of Nikolai Gogol*
David Copperfield by Charles Dickens

Ernest Hemingway was another writer fond of making 'best of' lists and frequently handed out reading advice. In a 1935 article for *Esquire* magazine – in which he suggests that writing about shooting is actually more enjoyable than shooting itself – Hemingway names seventeen books he would rather read for the first time than have an annual income of a million dollars a year. These were:

Winesburg, Ohio by Sherwood Anderson
Wuthering Heights by Emily Brontë
The Brothers Karamazov by Fyodor Dostoyevsky
La Reine Margot by Alexandre Dumas
Madame Bovary by Gustave Flaubert
Far Away and Long Ago by W.H. Hudson
Dubliners by James Joyce
Buddenbrooks by Thomas Mann
La Maison Tellier by Guy de Maupassant
Hail and Farewell by George Moore
Le Rouge et le Noir by Stendhal (Marie-Henri Beyle)
La Chartreuse de Parme by Stendhal (Marie-Henri Beyle)

Anna Karenina by Leo Tolstoy
War and Peace by Leo Tolstoy
A Sportsman's Sketches by Ivan Turgenev
Adventures of Huckleberry Finn by Mark Twain
Autobiographies by W.B. Yeats

He also put together a slightly overlapping 'list of books any writer should have read as a part of his education' for his friend and protégé Arnold Samuelson, who wrote about their time together fishing and sailing in his early bibliomemoir *With Hemingway: A Year in Key West and Cuba*. 'Some may bore you,' wrote Hemingway, 'others might inspire you and others are so beautifully written they'll make you feel it's hopeless for you to try to write.'

Wuthering Heights by Emily Brontë
The Blue Hotel by Stephen Crane
The Open Boat by Stephen Crane
The Enormous Room by e.e. cummings
The Brothers Karamazov by Fyodor Dostoyevsky
Madame Bovary by Gustave Flaubert
Far Away and Long Ago by W.H. Hudson
The American by Henry James
Dubliners by James Joyce
Buddenbrooks by Thomas Mann
Of Human Bondage by Somerset Maugham
Hail and Farewell by George Moore
The Red and the Black by Stendhal (Marie-Henri Beyle)
Anna Karenina by Leo Tolstoy
War and Peace by Leo Tolstoy
The Oxford Book of English Verse

Chapter Five

UNWANTED

BURNT BY THE NAZIS

A *Farewell to Arms* by Ernest Hemingway
How I Became a Socialist by Helen Keller
The Iron Heel, *The Jacket* and *Martin Eden* by Jack London
Deutsche Ansprache: ein Appell an die Vernunft (An Appeal to Reason) by Thomas Mann
All Quiet on the Western Front by Erich Maria Remarque
The Outline of History by H.G. Wells
Monographs about Marc Chagall and Paul Klee
All works published before 1933 by Sigmund Freud, Bertolt Brecht, Stefan Zweig, John Dos Passos and thousands of others

No to decadence and moral corruption! Yes to decency and morality in family and state! I consign to the flames the writings of Heinrich Mann, Bertolt Brecht, Ernst Gläser, Erich Kästner.
Joseph Goebbels, 10 May 1933, Berlin

It is impossible to put together an exhaustive list of all the books burnt by the Nazis between 1933 (when burnings started in earnest) and 1945, but estimates put it at well over 4,000.

An initial blacklist was drawn up by German librarian Wolfgang Herrmann and a 1935 issue of *Die Bucherei*, the Nazi journal for lending libraries, featured a list of guidelines for deciding which books and writers were fit for the flames. This included anything written by Jewish authors (irrespective of the subject), all pacifist literature, all Marxist literature and anything by foreigners or German emigrants in a foreign country badmouthing the new Germany.

More specifically, anything supporting the Weimar Republic, primitive Darwinism, or encouraging decadent art was also doomed. Anything about sexuality or sex education was highly suspect. Nor did previous success count for anything; Jack London, especially his *The Call of the Wild*, was one of the most popular foreign authors before Hitler's rise to power but that was no protection for his books. Matthew Fishburn, author of *Burning Books*, argues that having your books burnt was actually 'a confirmation of a writer's importance and credentials'. Indeed, Oscar Maria Graf demanded his works join those of his compatriots after he was initially left off the early lists ('Burn me!' he demanded).

The most famous burning was organised for 10 May 1933. Books were not simply tossed on to the pile; there were also 'Fire Oaths' which were short statements read out explaining why certain works and authors had been selected. Remarque's *All Quiet on the Western Front*, a huge bestseller in Germany, was one of the works specifically singled out because of its 'literary betrayal of the soldiers of the World War'. Freud was also namechecked because of his 'soul-shredding overvaluation of sexual activity'.

Another Fire Oath accused journalist Alfred Kerr of

'the arrogant corruption of the German language' – how he and his family made their consequent escape from Germany to London is told in *When Hitler Stole Pink Rabbit* by his daughter Judith Kerr, author of the Mog stories and *The Tiger Who Came To Tea*.

In 1934, two public libraries were established in opposition to the burnings. The stock of both the German Freedom Library (Deutsche Freiheitsbibliothek) in Paris, and the American Library of Nazi-Banned Books in Brooklyn, New York, was made up of the works which were lost in the fires.

MOST-CHALLENGED BOOKS IN AMERICA

1. *Looking for Alaska* by John Green
2. *Fifty Shades of Grey* by E.L. James
3. *I Am Jazz* by Jessica Herthel and Jazz Jennings
4. *Beyond Magenta: Transgender Teens Speak Out* by Susan Kuklin
5. *The Curious Incident of the Dog in the Night-Time* by Mark Haddon
6. *The Holy Bible*
7. *Fun Home* by Alison Bechdel
8. *Habibi* by Craig Thompson
9. *Nasreen's Secret School: A True Story from Afghanistan* by Jeanette Winter
10. *Two Boys Kissing* by David Levithan

Throughout the year, the American Library Association (ALA) receives reports from libraries and schools about attempts to ban books in communities across the country. Since 1990, they have put together a list of the most-challenged books and the reasons why people wanted to censor them. The above is the most recent (at the time of writing) top ten.

The main reasons are 'offensive language', 'sexually explicit' and 'homosexuality', although 'poorly written' was one reason given for banning Fifty Shades of Grey and 'religious viewpoint' for getting rid of the Bible.

These books are in good company. The ALA also puts together a list of classics that have been challenged – it is hard to name a 20th-century major work which does not merit a mention on it. The Great Gatsby, by F. Scott Fitzgerald? Check. The Catcher in the Rye, by J.D. Salinger? Check. The Grapes of Wrath, by John Steinbeck? Check.

Overall, polls indicated that people are becoming keener on banning books – one showed that while in 2011 only 18 per cent of those questioned were in favour of bans, that had risen to 28 per cent in 2015. In particular, increasing numbers want to remove books that include witchcraft or sorcery, while a third do not think children should be able to get the Koran from their school library.

The ALA's commitment to making booklists is impressive. As well as these annual lists, it has also put together lists of the most frequently challenged books by decade. Here is the top ten for 1990 to 1999:

1. *Scary Stories* (series) by Alvin Schwartz
2. *Daddy's Roommate* by Michael Willhoite
3. *I Know Why the Caged Bird Sings* by Maya Angelou
4. *The Chocolate War* by Robert Cormier

5. *The Adventures of Huckleberry Finn* by Mark Twain
6. *Of Mice and Men* by John Steinbeck
7. *Forever* by Judy Blume
8. *Bridge to Terabithia* by Katherine Paterson
9. *Heather Has Two Mommies* by Leslea Newman
10. *The Catcher in the Rye* by J.D. Salinger

And for 2000–2009:

1. *Harry Potter* (series) by J.K. Rowling
2. *Alice* (series) by Phyllis Reynolds Naylor
3. *The Chocolate War* by Robert Cormier
4. *And Tango Makes Three* by Justin Richardson and Peter Parnell
5. *Of Mice and Men* by John Steinbeck
6. *I Know Why the Caged Bird Sings* by Maya Angelou
7. *Scary Stories* (series) by Alvin Schwartz
8. *His Dark Materials* (series) by Philip Pullman
9. *ttyl; ttfn; l8r g8r* (series) by Lauren Myracle
10. *The Perks of Being a Wallflower* by Stephen Chbosky

THE MOST-UNREAD BOOKS

Tsundoju: *A Japanese term for the habit of buying books, then leaving them unread in a pile.*

1. *Catch-22* by Joseph Heller
2. *The Lord of the Rings* by J.R.R. Tolkien
3. *Ulysses* by James Joyce
4. *Moby-Dick* by Herman Melville
5. *Atlas Shrugged* by Ayn Rand

The constantly changing aspect of (not) reading books means that statistics on which ones are the most unread/ least finished are impossible to nail down once and for all. But we can see snapshots in time. Above, for example, are the top five Most Abandoned Classics as indicated by the members of Goodreads in July 2013. Below is its overall list of Most Abandoned:

1. *The Casual Vacancy* by J.K. Rowling
2. *Fifty Shades of Grey* by E.L. James
3. *Eat, Pray, Love* by Elizabeth Gilbert
4. *The Girl with the Dragon Tattoo* by Stieg Larsson
5. *Wicked* by Gregory Maguire

One, only half-serious, way of calculating unreadativity is the Hawking Index put together by maths professor Jordan Ellenberg, which analyses data from Kindles based upon how near the end of the book people highlighted a passage. On this basis the top five looks more like this (at least in July 2014), with figures in brackets indicating the percentage of people who got all the way through:

1. *Hard Choices* by Hilary Clinton (1.9%)
2. *Capital* by Thomas Piketty (2.4%)
3. *Infinite Jest* by David Foster Wallace (6.4%)
4. *A Brief History of Time* by Stephen Hawking (6.6%)
5. *Thinking, Fast and Slow* by Daniel Kahneman (6.8%)

Fifty Shades of Grey by E.L. James comes in at 25.9% and, perhaps surprisingly, this approach also suggests that 98.5% of people finished *The Goldfinch* by Donna Tartt.

Going further back, Malcolm Cowley, of *The New Republic* magazine, took a different approach to the issue. In 1934 he asked various well-known American novelists and literary critics to suggest books that not enough people knew about. He collated the results in two articles, 'Good Books That Almost Nobody Has Read' and 'More About Neglected Books'. These were F. Scott Fitzgerald's five choices (though he also mentioned the crime fiction of Raoul Whitfield):

Through the Wheat by Thomas Boyd
Sing Before Breakfast by Vincent McHugh
The Spring Flight by Lee J. Smits
Miss Lonelyhearts by Nathanael West
I Thought of Daisy by Edmund Wilson

A fine place to track down forgotten books is neglectedbooks.com, which features 'articles and lists with thousands of books that have been neglected, overlooked, forgotten or stranded by changing tides in critical or popular taste'. It features a long list of Lists of Neglected Books and a separate section on Justly Neglected ones.

JOE ORTON'S DAMAGED BOOKS

The Dog Beneath the Skin by W.H. Auden and Christopher Isherwood
Easy Come Easy Go by James Hadley Chase
Poirot Investigates by Agatha Christie
The Secret of Chimneys by Agatha Christie
The Lunts by George Freedley

The Great Tudors edited by Katherine Garvin
Queen's Favourite by Phyllis Hambledon
Three Men and Jennie by Naomi Jacob
Exotic Cage Birds by Marcel Legendre
The World of Paul Sickey by John Osborne
Collins Guide to Roses by Bertram Park
Steel Cocoon by Bentz Plagemann
Death Takes a Partner by John Rhode
Clouds of Witness by Dorothy L. Sayers
All's Well That Ends Well, Antony and Cleopatra, Cymbeline,
    Julius Caesar, King Henry IV Parts 1 and 2, King Henry VIII,
    King Henry V, King John, King Lear, King Richard II, Macbeth,
    Othello, The Tempest, Timon of Athens, Titus Andronicus by
    William Shakespeare
John Betjeman by Derek Stanford
Golk by Richard G. Stern
The Three Faces of Eve by Corbet H. Thigpen and Hervery
    M. Cleckley
Alec Clunes by J.C. Trewin
Sybil Thorndike by J.C. Trewin
Robert Helpmann by Kathrine Sorley Walker
The Collected Plays of Emlyn Williams
Yoga and Health by Selvarajan Yesudian and Elisabeth Haich
Seen Any Good Films Lately? by William K. Zinsser

> 'Libraries might as well not exist; they've got endless shelves
> for rubbish and hardly any space for good books.'
> Joe Orton

Pinching books from libraries has a long history, as does straightforward library-book vandalism. The most high-profile 20th-century perpetrators were playwright Joe Orton and his partner Kenneth Halliwell who, from January 1959 until 1962, defaced the covers of various books in Islington Public Library. They only stopped when they were discovered and given a six-month prison sentence for theft and malicious damage and a fine of £262.

While they simply removed some plates from art books to use as decoration in their flat, most of their work involved adding incongruous images of people (especially heads), animals and objects to the covers, although occasionally they also adjusted the text and pasted in lewd blurbs. This 'guerrilla artwork' was then returned to the shelves. 'I used to stand in the corners after I'd smuggled the doctored books back into the library and then watch people read them,' said Orton. 'It was very fun, very interesting.'

Examples of the defacement include the addition of two smartly dressed cats to the front cover of The Secret of Chimneys by Agatha Christie, a tattooed and all but naked middle-aged man on the dustjacket of a selection of John Betjeman poems, and a new blurb for Clouds of Witness by Dorothy Sayers that would make most regular library users blush.

Orton and Halliwell were eventually charged with stealing seventy-two books and removing 1,653 plates from art books. Their work is now held by the Islington Local History Centre and is on show in the Islington Museum.

MOST POPULAR OUT-OF-PRINT BOOKS

1. *Westworld* by Michael Crichton
2. *Sex* by Madonna
3. *Permaculture: A Designers' Manual* by Bill Mollison
4. *Unintended Consequences* by John Ross
5. *Encyclopedia of Pieced Quilt Patterns* by Barbara Brackman
6. *Finding the Winning Edge* by Bill Walsh
7. *Mastering Atmosphere & Mood in Watercolor* by Joseph Zbukvic
8. *Fast Times at Ridgemont High* by Cameron Crowe
9. *Margin of Risk: Risk-Averse Value Investing Strategies for the Thoughtful Investor* by Seth Klarman
10. *Alla Prima: Everything I Know about Painting* by Richard Schmid
11. *Rage* by Richard Bachman (Stephen King)
12. *The Vision and Beyond: Prophecies Fulfilled and Still to Come* by David Wilkerson
13. *Sled Driver: Flying the World's Fastest Jet* by Brian Shul
14. *Bandit Country: The IRA and South Armagh* by Toby Harnden
15. *Snake* by Ken Stabler
16. *Halloween* by Curtis Richards
17. *Parts Work: An Illustrated Guide to Your Inner Life* by Tom Holmes
18. *Promise Me Tomorrow* by Nora Roberts
19. *Portrait of a Killer: Jack the Ripper – Case Closed* by Patricia Cornwell
20. *Down Through the Years* by Jean Shepard

Since 2003, BookFinder.com has been issuing an annual list of the most searched-for out-of-print books in the USA. This most recent top twenty features many regulars from previous lists, in particular Madonna's limited edition of erotic exploration, and Stephen King's nom-de-plume novel about a school shooting, which he himself requested not be reprinted to prevent copycat violence.

Another perennial favourite is Promise Me Tomorrow by romance novelist Nora Roberts, who has sold millions of books but, as do many critics, regards this volume of her work as an absolute stinker and, in her own words, 'full of clichés'. She does not want to see it back in print (which consequently means it is now collectable and expensive to buy). Here's the blurb:

> Sarah had to build something major, in her work and in her life.
> And Byron's searing kiss stirred wild longings in her no other man
> had roused. Her future as an architect was in his hands. But he
> would trap her in a desperate passion, one never fulfilled by love.
> She fled to a glamorous assignment in Paris, to the embrace of an
> elegant Frenchman whose sensuous caress hid a dangerous ambition.
> Then destiny brought Byron into her life again, tempting her with
> new dreams, drawing her into the flames of the one unforgettable love
> that promised to consume her, body, heart and soul.

The list also reflects currently successful films and television programmes. HBO's popular new take on Michael Crichton's Westworld resulted in a huge uptick in interest in the original robo-western book – a 1974 companion to the 1973 Yul Brynner film, including a script rather than a novelisation, plus black and white photos – propelling it to the top of the chart.

Often there or thereabouts on the lists is *Fast Times at Ridgemont High* by Cameron Crowe, his book about an undercover year at Clairemont High School which was the basis of the screenplay for the successful film of the same name in 1982. But as well as regulars, there are often themes to the searches. The year 2010 saw plenty of titles focusing on home improvements following the previous year's fall-out from the stock market crash, when books about personal finance and economics had dominated the list.

Later lists have lumped all the books together in a top 100 rundown, but in the early years they were split up into various subcategories such as history, fiction and poetry. In the Mysteries and Thrillers section, Rex Stout held the top four places (*Where There's a Will*, *The Rubber Band*, *The Red Box* and *The League of Frightened Men*). The top ten in the first-ever children's category, released in 2003 were, in declining order of demand:

1. *Northern Lights* by Philip Pullman
2. *Oddkins: A Fable For All Ages* by Dean Koontz
3. *Our Island Story: A History of England for Boys and Girls* by Henrietta Elizabeth Marshall
4. *The Book of Indians* by Holling Clancy Holling
5. *Miss Suzy* by Miriam Young
6. *The Book of Cowboys* by Holling Clancy Holling
7. *Boobsey Twins at the Seashore* by Laura Lee Hope
8. *Uncle Arthur's Bedtime Stories* by Arthur S. Maxwell
9. *Under the Window* by Kate Greenaway
10. *Little Pictures of Japan* by Olive Beaupré Miller

BANNED BOOKS AT GUANTÁNAMO DETAINEE LIBRARY

Money by Martin Amis

The New Dinkum Aussie Dictionary by R. Beckett

The Rule of Law by Lord Thomas Bingham

Booky Wook Two by Russell Brand

Blasphemy: How the Religious Right is Hijacking Our Declaration of Independence by Alan Dershowitz

The African American Slave by Frederick Douglass

The Kill List by Frederick Forsyth

I'm Not the Only One by George Galloway

Blair's Wars by John Kampfner

Futility by Wilfred Owen

Hidden Agendas by John Pilger

The Merchant of Venice by William Shakespeare

An Honourable Deception: New Labour, Iraq and the Misuse of Power by Clare Short

Gulag Archipelago by Aleksandr Solzhenitsyn

Bad Men by Clive Stafford Smith

Injustice by Clive Stafford Smith

Uncle Tom's Cabin by Harriet Beecher Stowe

Presumed Innocent by Scott Turow

Puss in Boots

Cinderella

Jack and the Beanstalk

Beauty and the Beast

The Bible

It stocks around 20,000 books in eighteen different languages. J.K. Rowling, Agatha Christie and J.R.R. Tolkien are among its most popular authors. And it has the most unfathomable accession process of any library in the world.

There is no official list of proscribed books at the Guantánamo Detainee Library. Decisions are made on a book-by-book basis after each volume is read by two officials. However, there are guidelines in place, partly to ensure that prisoners don't use books to communicate. The kind of books that fall under the heading 'Authorised' feature 'Themes of family, tolerance, moral choices, mental escape, topics that expand the mind'. There is then a general list of restrictions which covers 'topics with potential to create controversy or to train in ways to fight'. As well as banning classified advertisements and travel offers, this covers:

Extremism
Militant religious ideologies
Racial and cultural hate groups' ideologies (e.g. anti-American, anti-Semitic, anti-Western)
Military topics
Excessive graphic violence
Sexual situation (nudity, ads for sexual enhancement substances and/or treating sexual dysfunctions)
Physical geography (e.g. plans of buildings or subway systems that provide information about targets of potential attacks)

This list of banned books is an ongoing compilation by Clive Stafford Smith, director of the charity Reprieve, which concentrates on legal support for people facing the death penalty or held in secret prisons. These are the books that he has not been allowed to give to clients. In addition to this list, Mohamedou Ould Slahi has not been allowed to receive a copy of his memoir *Guantánamo Diary*. Similarly, *Poems from Guantánamo: The Detainees Speak*, a collection of poems written by detainees, has not made it on to the library's shelves.

It is not easy to see a pattern – George Orwell's *1984* and *Animal Farm* have both got in, as has Kafka's *The Trial* – and decisions can be overturned. After a campaign via the pages of the *New York Times*, John Grisham managed to get the ban on his books *The King of Torts* and *The Innocent Man* rescinded (although Frederick Forsyth has said it is a badge of honour to be banned in Guantánamo Bay). Initially, neither Samuel Beckett's *Waiting for Godot* nor Dostoyevsky's *Crime and Punishment* were allowed in, but the 'Gitmobooks' photo collection tumblr which charts the library's contents shows that they are both now available. One theme that Stafford Smith says he has identified is that it seems to be the censor's view that Guantánamo detainees should not be allowed any materials that would help them learn English.

Vice magazine has added a few more titles which appear also to be banned to the list:

A Most Wanted Man by John Le Carré
Cruel Britannia: A Secret History of Torture by Ian Cobain
Interventions by Noam Chomsky (a collection of opinion
    pieces)
The Diary of a Young Girl by Anne Frank
Trainspotting by Irvine Welsh
A People's History of the United States by Howard Zinn

Chapter Six
ON THE SCREEN

BIG BANG THEORY: THE ART
OF THE TELEVISION BOOKSHELF

Perspectives of Modern Physics by Arthur Beiser

Handbook of Physics by Walter Benenson et al.

Perspectives in Nuclear Physics at Intermediate Energies edited
  by Sigfrido Boffi et al.

The Particle Explosion by Frank Close et al.

Low Temperature Physics by Christian Enss

Fundamentals of Physics (3rd edition) by David Halliday and
  Robert Resnick

Nonlinear Methods of Spectral Analysis edited by Simon Haykin

The Nature of Solids by Alan Holden

Thermal Physics by Charles Kittel

Electron-Molecule Collisions and Photoionization Processes by
  Vincent McKoy

Nuclear Forces by Leon Rosenfeld

Physics of Solids under High Pressure by James Schilling and
  Robert Shelton

Fundamentals of X-Ray and Radium Physics by Joseph Selman

*College Physics Fifth Edition, Study Guide and Student Solutions
  Manual* by Raymond Serway et al.

New Problems in the Physics of Glass by Vasiliĭ Vasil'evich Tarasov
Applied Elasticity by Chi-teh Wang
The World of Physics by Jefferson Weaver
Physics of the Atom by Mentzer Wehr and James Richards
Light Scattering Spectra of Solids: Proceedings of the
   International Conference Held at New York University, New
   York, September 3–6, edited by George Wright
University Physics by Hugh Young and Roger Freedman

Designers and prop masters put a tremendous amount of thought into building the sets of television shows. But it's not just about the sofas and lamps; it's also important to choose the right books to suit the characters.

Occasionally, most viewers will spot a book they recognise on screen, but some fans go several steps further than that, using their pause button to examine fictional bookcases, desks and entire series in forensic detail. The list above represents only those books in *The Big Bang Theory* on the shelves in Sheldon's and Leonard's sitting room which are about physics. There are separate sections listed on the *Big Bang Theory* wiki for many other subjects including chemistry, nuclear engineering and fiction.

Similarly Mary Jo Watts has painstakingly put together various lists for BBC's *Sherlock* series, which not only document what's on show at 221B Baker Street (drilling down to specific locations such as 'On Sherlock's desk' at her site at mid0nz.wordpress.com) but also by episode. Interesting volumes include *Moriarty's Police Law* by W.J. Williams and a first edition of Goethe's *Faust* in German.

As well as owning books, characters sometimes even read them. There are plenty of literary references in

Friends, including the episode in which Phoebe manages to convince Rachel that Jane Eyre is a cyborg. Here is every book that we see being read on screen in all ten seasons of *Friends*:

Little Women by Louisa May Alcott (Joey)
Wuthering Heights by Emily Brontë (Phoebe)
Chicken Soup for the Soul by Jack Canfield (Chandler)
The Shining by Stephen King (Rachel)
What to Expect When You're Expecting by Heidi Murkoff (Joey, somewhat surprisingly)
Race: How Blacks and Whites Think and Feel About The American Obsession by Studs Terkel (Ross)

Monica's boyfriend Julio reads Baudelaire's *Les Fleurs du mal*, but sadly the scriptwriters made up the feminist bestseller *Be Your Own Windkeeper* which Monica and Phoebe introduce to Rachel.

One of the series with the highest book count is *Gilmore Girls*, largely because the lead character Rory is a big reader. There is even a special Rory Gilmore Reading Challenge in which fans aim to read each of the 339 books read or mentioned in the series. Here's what she says in her valedictorian speech:

> I live in two worlds, one is a world of books. I've been a resident of Faulkner's Yoknapatawpha County, hunted the white whale aboard the Pequod, fought alongside Napoleon, sailed a raft with Huck and Jim, committed absurdities with Ignatius J. Reilly, rode a sad train with Anna Karenina and strolled down Swann's Way.

The Simpsons, America's longest-running sitcom, also has an impressive book list pedigree, largely thanks to Lisa's devotion to the written word. The Lisa Simpson Book Club (online at lisasimpsonbookclub.tumblr.com) charts references to works of literature on the show in general and Lisa's personal picks, which include *The Bell Jar* by Sylvia Plath, *The Elegant Universe* by Brian Greene and *The Brothers Karamazov* by Fyodor Dostoevsky.

THE DEAD POETS SOCIETY POEMS

'She Walks in Beauty' by Lord Byron
'The Ballad of William Bloat' by Raymond Calvert
'The Prophet' by Abraham Cowley
'The Road Not Taken' by Robert Frost
'To the Virgins' by Robert Herrick
'The Congo' by Vachel Lindsay
'Shall I Compare Thee to a Summer's Day' by William
    Shakespeare
A Midsummer Night's Dream by William Shakespeare
'Ulysses' by Alfred Lord Tennyson
'Walden' by Henry David Thoreau
'O Captain! My Captain!' by Walt Whitman
'O Me! O Life!' by Walt Whitman

Poems not only punctuate many successful films – such as W.H. Auden's 'Funeral Blues' in *Four Weddings and a Funeral* and Thomas Hardy's 'Drummer Hodge' in *The History Boys* – they sometimes even provide the title itself, as Alexander Pope's 'Eloisa to Abelard' does for the 2004 film *Eternal*

Sunshine of the Spotless Mind. In *A Matter of Life and Death* (1946) the central character, played by David Niven, is an RAF pilot who is also a poet, given to quoting Andrew Marvell and Walter Raleigh ('I'd rather have written that than flown through Hitler's legs') and the film ends with Sir Walter Scott on love:

> Love rules the court, the camp, the grove,
> And men below and saints above;
> For love is heaven, and heaven is love.

Lord Byron's 'She Walks in Beauty Like the Night' also makes an appearance in the film, as it does in *Dead Poets Society* starring Robin Williams and Ethan Hawke. It is one of the poems that Charlie/Nuwanda recites and passes off as his own to the girls he invites to a meeting of the reformed DPS in the cave (the other is 'Shall I Compare Thee to a Summer's Day?'). The cave is also the location for Neil's effort at Tennyson and Meeks's atmospheric chanting recitation of performance poet Vachel Lindsay's 'The Congo':

> Then I had religion, then I had a vision
> I could not turn from their revel in derision
> Then I saw the Congo, creeping through the black
> Cutting through the jungle with a golden track.

Not all the poems are widely known. Charlie's commentary on a Playboy centrefold ('Teach me to Love? Go teach thy self more wit') comes from Abraham Cowley's *The Prophet*, while the rather bloodthirsty 'The Ballad of William Bloat' with its twist in the tale ('In a mean abode in the Shankhill Road') probably passes many viewers by. More familiar works include 'To the Virgins' by Robert Herrick, whose 'gather ye rosebuds' philosophy is the central concept of the film, 'Walden' by Henry David Thoreau (all meetings of the original DPS started 'I went to the woods because I wished to live deliberately') and, inevitably, 'The Road Not Taken' by Robert Frost from his collection *Mountain Interval*. But the backbone of the film is Walt Whitman. Robin Williams's teacher Mr Keating slightly abridges 'O me! O Life!' to explain the purpose of poetry to his pupils:

> Oh me! Oh life! of the questions of these recurring,
> Of the endless trains of the faithless, of cities fill'd with the foolish.

He even suggests to the boys that they should call him Captain, as they all do at the close of the film when the fearful trip is indeed done.

THE WRATH OF KHAN: A STAR TREK BOOKSHELF

Inferno by Dante Alighieri
A Tale of Two Cities by Charles Dickens
Moby-Dick by Herman Melville
Paradise Lost (two copies) by John Milton
Paradise Regained by John Milton
King Lear by William Shakespeare
Statute Regulating [Interplanetary Commerce?]
The Bible

Star Trek: The Wrath of Khan (1982) is not renowned for its snazzy special effects, but it is indisputably the most literary of all the spin-off films from the television series. Both the film's writer/director Nicholas Meyer and *Star Trek*'s original creator Gene Roddenberry have talked about seeing the series specifically as the continuing mission of Horatio Hornblower in space.

So when we come across Khan Noonien Singh's presence in the film for the first time it is no surprise that he is represented by his bookshelf (contents detailed above) from his ship the *Botany Bay*. The titles are carefully chosen and indicate aspects of Khan's character or play a key part in the film. Meyer says that he built Khan's character on the basis that while he was feeding his discontent and biding his time during exile on Ceti Alpha V, he would have been reading.

Khan is portrayed as a fallen angel/Satan (*Inferno*), a superior but rebellious being undergoing considerable suffering and punishment. Before the film begins, he has already been exiled by Captain Kirk to a desolate planet in the television series episode when we first meet him, 'Space Seed' (1967). Even at this early meeting, Khan mentions Milton and Kirk specifically comments on: 'the statement Lucifer made when he fell into the pit, "It is better to rule in hell than serve in heaven".' Khan's new home, Ceti Alpha V, has become a very hell, hot, arid and full of monsters. Meanwhile, Kirk is having a King Lear moment, worried about ageing, dealing with retirement and relationships with his offspring, as well as haunted by poor life choices.

Some critics have gone further and argued that the

Enterprise represents heaven, which is run by a kind of trinity of Kirk, Spock and Dr McCoy. Spock is certainly portrayed as a Christ figure in the film, redeeming the 'world' and then 'resurrected' in the following movie. The concept of resurrection is also central to another key text to *Wrath of Khan*, Charles Dickens's *A Tale of Two Cities*. In an early scene, Spock gives Kirk a copy as a birthday present. Kirk reads aloud the iconic 'It was the best of times, it was the worst of times' line and by the end Spock has fully become Carton, giving his life so that Kirk (Darnay, in this sense) can live. As the film ends, Kirk goes into recitative mode again to add: 'It is a far, far better thing that I do, than I have ever done. It is a far, far better rest I go to, than I have ever known.' Moreover, Carton is shown as living on in a spiritual sense and Spock via his spiritual essence, his 'katra'. This endures thanks to his mind-meld with McCoy before returning fully in *The Search for Spock*.

Most of all, this is a film about obsession. The driving text is *Moby-Dick* and the frenzied search for revenge which consumes Khan as he aims to spear Kirk. Like Kirk, Khan quotes directly from the source. His final utterance is 'From Hell's heart, I stab at thee, for hate's sake I spit my last breath at thee', but before then he has also pledged that 'I'll chase him around the Moons of Nibia and round the Antares maelstrom, and around Perdition's flames before I give him up', in much the same way that Ahab says of the whale that 'I'll chase him round Good Hope, and round the Horn, and round the Norway Maelstrom, and round Perdition's flames before I give him up'.

A GOOD WILL HUNTING HISTORIOGRAPHY

Manufacturing Consent by Noam Chomsky
*The Best Poor Man's Country: A Geographical Study of Early
    Southeastern Pennsylvania* by Dr James T. Lemon
*Farmers and Fishermen: Two Centuries of Work in Essex County,
    Massachusetts, 1630–1850* by Daniel Vickers
The Radicalism of the American Revolution by Dr Gordon S.
    Wood
A People's History of the United States by Howard Zinn

Matt Damon's eponymous character in Good Will Hunting is not merely a mathematical genius (although to be honest the problem he solves in the film is not that hard), he's also a heavy reader who is shown speed-reading a psychology book before chucking it in the bin. Indeed, the list of writers he name-checks when his therapist Sean Maguire (Robin Williams) asks for his favourites includes Shakespeare, Nietzsche, Frost, [perhaps Flannery?] O'Connor, Chaucer, Pope and Kant (at which point Sean points out that they are all dead). Earlier in the film, Will also picks Oscar Wilde and Gertrude Stein when he tries to annoy the psychologist whose book he has just binned.

More specifically, Will tells Sean in no uncertain terms that, 'If you wanna read a real history book, read Howard Zinn's *A People's History of the United States*.' Matt Damon knew Zinn well and is obviously an admirer of his approach (you can see a clip on YouTube of the actor reading from Zinn's speech 'The Problem is Civil Obedience'). His History is a revisionist look at America from 1492 to the present day, arguing that the working class – of which Will Hunting is a member – has been economically exploited by a ruling minority for centuries. For reasons that are not entirely clear, Will is less keen on Sean's suggested reading matter of Noam Chomsky's *Manufacturing Consent*, which takes a very critical look at propaganda and the role of the media in America. 'You people baffle me,' he says. 'You spend all this money on beautiful, fancy books and they're the wrong ******* books.'

History, and of the more radical persuasion, is obviously a preoccupation of Will's. In the scene where he meets his future girlfriend Skylar (Minnie Driver) in a bar, he puts down a smart-alec Harvard student who is trying to show off his knowledge of colonial American historiography. In doing so he cites various authorities on the subject of capitalism and inequality in that period:

> You're a first year grad student. You just finished some Marxian historian, Pete Garrison[1] probably, and so naturally that's what you believe until next month when you get to James Lemon[2] and get convinced that Virginia and Pennsylvania were strongly entrepreneurial and capitalist back in 1740. That'll last until sometime in your second year, then you'll be in here regurgitating Gordon Wood[3] about the pre-revolutionary utopia and the capital-forming effects of military mobilisation ... You got that from 'Work in Essex County'[4] page 421, right? Do you have any thoughts of your own on the subject or were you just gonna plagiarise the whole book for me?

Notes

1 A fictitious Marxist historian.

2 Dr James T. Lemon is a specialist in urban historical geography who turned his doctoral dissertation on 18th-century

settlements in Pennsylvania into *The Best Poor Man's Country: A Geographical Study of Early Southeastern Pennsylvania*, and was awarded the Albert J. Beveridge Award in 1972 by the American Historical Association for the best book on American history.

3 Dr Gordon S. Wood is Professor of History Emeritus at Brown University. He won the 1993 Pulitzer Prize for History for *The Radicalism of the American Revolution*.

4 *Farmers and Fishermen: Two Centuries of Work in Essex County, Massachusetts*, 1630–1850 was written by Dr Daniel Vickers and in 1995 won the American Historical Association's John H. Dunning Prize for the best book on any subject pertaining to the history of the United States.

MURPH'S INTERSTELLAR BOOKSHELF

Flatland: A Romance of Many Dimensions by Edwin Abbott
Little Women by Louisa May Alcott
Time's Arrow by Martin Amis
The Balloon Man by Charlotte Armstrong
Emma by Jane Austen
The Wasp Factory by Iain Banks
Lindbergh by A. Scott Berg
Labyrinths by Jorge Luis Borges
The Good Earth by Pearl S. Buck
The Reapers by John Connolly
Zeitoun by Dave Eggers
The Waste Land by T.S. Eliot
The Big Nowhere by James Ellroy
The Devil's Alternative by Frederick Forsyth

In a Different Voice: Psychological Theory and Women's Development by Carol Gilligan
The Fault in Our Stars by John Green
The Go-Between by L.P. Hartley
Winter's Tale by Mark Helprin
The Fatal Shore by Robert Hughes
The Century by Peter Jennings and Todd Brewster
The Stand by Stephen King
A Wrinkle in Time by Madeleine L'Engle
The Willoughbys by Lois Lowry
Moby-Dick by Herman Melville
One Hundred Years of Solitude by Gabriel Garcia Marquez
Maugham: A Biography by Ted Morgan
Three Cups of Tea by Greg Mortenson and David Oliver Relin
Gravedigger's Daughter by Joyce Carol Oates
We were the Mulvaneys by Joyce Carol Oates
Downwinders: An Atomic Tale by Curtis and Diane Oberhansly
A Life Inspired: Tales of the Peace Corps by Peace Corps
Little Children by Tom Perrotta
Gravity's Rainbow by Thomas Pynchon
The Fountainhead by Ayn Rand
Wonderstruck by Brian Selznick
The Glass Castle by Jeannette Walls
The Time Machine by H.G. Wells
Out of the Blue by Isabel Wolff
The Story of Edgar Sawtelle: A Novel (P.S.) by David Wroblewski
Roget's Thesaurus
Unabridged Dictionary of the English Language
The Official Scrabble Players Dictionary
Encyclopedia Britannica

*** Minor spoilers alert ***

There are many bookcases in films but none like the one in Christopher Nolan's science-fiction masterpiece *Interstellar*. He is an English literature graduate of University College London, and much of his work centres on the nature of time; so it is only natural that the bookcase in Murph's bedroom, which plays a key role in the film, is stocked with appropriate titles.

This is such an important element in many television shows and films that the Strand Bookstore in New York has a special service to supply titles which fit the bill – so, for example, the bookshelves in *Indiana Jones and the Kingdom of the Crystal Skull* are heavy on palaeontology, marine biology and pre-Columbian society, and all the books were published before 1957 when the film is set.

Many of the *Interstellar* titles have been identified by a variety of eagle-eyed viewers and are collected above. Among the key texts are *The Stand* (set in a post-apocalyptic future and featuring the decidedly time-non-lineal character Randall Flagg), *A Wrinkle in Time* (which Nolan has credited as inspiring his interest in higher dimensions and the idea of a tesseract), and *Winter's Tale* (which begins 'I have been to another world, and come back. Listen to me.'). The chronological jiggery-pokery of *Time's Arrow* is also of obvious relevance.

None, though, is more important than *Flatland*, which is all about understanding the existence of multiple dimensions (*** biggish spoiler alert ***): it is also the book pushed out by Cooper from the tesseract when he shouts at himself not to leave Earth.

Among the authors represented on the bookcase is Isabel Wolff, who had no idea her novel *Out of the Blue*, a romantic comedy about fidelity in friendship and relationships, would feature in the film until she was watching it in the cinema. It is one of the most visible titles and Wolff admits she was delighted to see it, but has no idea why it was included.

Chapter Seven
LISTS YET TO COME

FUTURE CLASSICS

Noughts and Crosses by Malorie Blackman
The Boy in the Striped Pyjamas by John Boyne
How to Train Your Dragon by Cressida Cowell
The Gruffalo's Child by Julia Donaldson and Axel Scheffler
The Curious Incident of the Dog in the Night-Time by
   Mark Haddon
Private Peaceful by Michael Morpurgo
The Amber Spyglass by Philip Pullman
Harry Potter and the Deathly Hallows by J.K. Rowling
Harry Potter and the Order of the Phoenix by J.K. Rowling
Harry Potter and the Half-Blood Prince by J.K. Rowling

It's a brave soothsayer who claims to know what we will be reading next year, let alone to predict the books that will become classics and the authors who will stand the test of time. Readers in the USA of the popular quarterly magazine *The Colophon* made a stab in 1936 at guessing the ten authors whose works would be regarded as classics in 2000. They put Sinclair Lewis in the top spot, followed by Willa Cather, Eugene O'Neill and Edna St. Vincent Millay.

The rest of the top ten were:

5. Robert Frost
6. Theodore Dreiser
7. James Truslow Adams
8. George Santayana
9. Stephen Vincent Benet
10. James Branch Cabell

A survey of more than 7,000 readers in 2016 by National Book Tokens as part of World Book Day showed that when it comes to favourite heroes and worst villains, there is a large faction cheering on Roald Dahl and J.K. Rowling (although the over-45s put in a strong word for the likes of Jo March and Paddington Bear). The top ten 21st-century children's books most likely to become classics are listed above, though a separate list chosen by under-16s would have included *Gangsta Granny* by David Walliams and *Diary of a Wimpy Kid* by Jeff Kinney.

The online news site Mic, established in 2011 and squarely targeted at millennials, suggests a different selection will be the ones taught in schools in the future:

The Brief Wondrous Life of Oscar Wao by Junot Díaz
A Visit from the Goon Squad by Jennifer Egan
Middlesex by Jeffrey Eugenides
Freedom by Jonathan Franzen
The Kite Runner by Khaled Hosseini
The Namesake by Jhumpa Lahiri
Life of Pi by Yann Martel
Dear Life by Alice Munro

Gilead by Marilynne Robinson
Tenth of December by George Saunders
White Teeth by Zadie Smith

Of course publishers have an obvious interest in this parlour game too. In 2008, Gollancz, the science-fiction and fantasy imprint of Orion, reissued eight of its titles under the banner of 'Future Classics' (and, slightly disconcertingly, with covers lacking both the name of the book or author). Here they are:

Evolution by Stephen Baxter
Blood Music by Greg Bear
Schild's Ladder by Greg Egan
Fairyland by Paul J. McAuley
Altered Carbon by Richard Morgan
The Separation by Christopher Priest
Revelation Space by Alastair Reynolds
Hyperion by Dan Simmons

FUTURE LIBRARY

Scribbler Moon by Margaret Atwood
From Me Flows What You Call Time by David Mitchell
Untitled by Sjón

At the end of *Orlando*, Virginia Woolf's hero/ine considers burying his/her poem 'The Oak Tree' in the roots of the original tree that inspired it. As Orlando puts it, this would be returning to the land what it has given her/him.

Books are popular deposits in time capsules. More than 200 works of fiction and hundreds of reference books and textbooks ('authoritative books on every subject of importance known to mankind') were sealed inside 'The Crypt of Civilisation' at Oglethorpe University in Atlanta, Georgia, in 1940. What the residents of Earth will make of them when it is opened in May 8113 is anybody's guess.

However, artist Katie Paterson's project Framtidsbiblioteket, or Future Library, puts the books centre stage, fusing notions of writing and survival as did Woolf's *Orlando*. It aims to examine ecology, environment and the inter-connectedness of things, while questioning people's inclination towards short-term thinking.

So every year, a new writer hands over an unpublished text which is stored in a specially designed room in the Deichmanske Public Library in Oslo until 2114 when they will be made available to the public for the first time and printed as an anthology. Margaret Atwood was the first choice, followed by David Mitchell, then in 2017 Icelandic novelist Sjón, who describes it as 'a game played on the grandest of scales'. Around 1,000 trees have been planted in the forest of Nordmarka near Oslo to ensure that there will be enough paper to print it. Wood from the forest will also be used to line the special reading room. 'How strange it is to think of my own voice silent by then for a long time suddenly being awakened,' said Margaret Atwood.

David Mitchell said that when he was first asked to take part he thought it was a mad idea, then that it was 'good mad', and finally that it was quite liberating. 'The project is a vote of confidence that, despite the catastrophist shadows under which we live, the future will still be a brightish place willing and able to complete an artistic endeavour begun by long-dead people a century ago,' he said.

A special ceremony is held in the forest each spring to mark the handover of the author's text, none of which have been discussed with nor shown to anybody else. A video of Margaret Atwood's ceremony is available at vimeo.com/135817557.

'Future Library is a living, breathing, organic artwork, unfolding over 100 years,' says Katie Paterson. 'It will live and breathe through the material growth of the trees. I imagine the tree rings as chapters in a book. The unwritten words, year by year, activated, materialised.'

Keep checking back on www.futurelibrary.no for updates on the project over the coming decades.

Chapter Eight

ADVENTURES IN BOOKS

EVERYTHING IN SHAVIAN

Alice's Adventures in Wonderland by Lewis Carroll
Androcles and the Lion by George Bernard Shaw
The Dhammapada edited by Tim Brown
Poe meets Shaw edited by Tim Brown
Classics of Men's Rights edited by Tim Brown

This is one of the shorter lists in the book, yet it is also the most comprehensive as it contains every book published in the Shavian alphabet.

Playwright and cultural commentator George Bernard Shaw found English a cumbersome language in which to craft his work, so the first draft of all his plays was written in the phonetically based Pitman shorthand before being transcribed using a typewriter.

Shaw served from 1926 to 1939 on the BBC's Spoken English Advisory Committee and by 1941 some of his thoughts about a solution to the perceived difficulty of the English alphabet were beginning to crystallise. That year, in the preface to Richard Albert Wilson's book *The Miraculous Birth of Language*, Shaw wrote that he wanted to see 'an alphabet capable of representing the sounds of the following string of nonsense quite unequivocally without using two letters to represent one sound or making the same letter represent different sounds by diacritical marks'. Shaw also wrote a letter to the *Times* on the subject and began a campaign to make it happen. 'Let people spell as they speak,' he said, 'without any nonsense about bad or good or right or wrong spelling and speech.'

And so in his 1950 will, he made provision for a trust and an international competition to design a new, more consistent, alphabet which would simplify written/ printed English and which had to:

- contain at least forty letters, each representing one sound only;
- be as phonetic as possible;
- be unlike the Latin alphabet.

'The only danger I can foresee in the establishment of an English alphabet,' he wrote, phlegmatically, 'is the danger of civil war.'

There were four winners of the competition and they were then merged by designer Ronald Kingsley Read into the Shavian or Shaw Alphabet. This is a mixture of tall, deep and short letters which represent consonants, nasals and vowels. They can also be rotated and some very common words, such as 'and', are also abbreviated as single letters. Although there are familiar word spaces and punctuation, there are no special upper or lower cases.

Because of various issues with Shaw's will, the Trust he set up to publicise the new alphabet only had enough funds to publish one of Shaw's plays, *Androcles and the Lion*, using the new alphabet. It appeared in 1962 in a Penguin parallel text edition with the original English.

Apart from a journal called *Shaw-Script* printed in Shavian in the 1960s, nothing further appeared for nearly fifty years until an edition of the works of Edgar Allan Poe in 2012, and the *Alice* transcription in 2013. There are also unpublished editions of J.K. Rowling's *Harry Potter and the Philosopher's Stone* and Ernest Hemingway's *The Old Man and the Sea* put together by enthusiasts for personal use.

The Powerhouse Museum in Sydney, Australia, holds one of the very few Shavian keyboard Imperial Good Companion Model 6 portable typewriters in existence, first made in the early 1960s.

BOOKS ANNOTATED BY DAVID FOSTER WALLACE

Players by Don DeLillo
Ratner's Star by Don DeLillo
The Silence of the Lambs by Thomas Harris
Carrie by Stephen King
The Lion, The Witch and the Wardrobe by C.S. Lewis
Suttree by Cormac McCarthy
The Puttermesser Papers by Cynthia Ozick
The Man Who Loved Children by Christina Stead
Rabbit, Run by John Updike
Borges: A Life by Edwin Williamson

> In getting my books, I have always been solicitous of an ample
> margin; this is not so much through any love of the thing in itself,
> however agreeable, as for the facility it affords me of penciling in
> suggested thoughts, agreements, and differences of opinion, or brief
> critical comments in general.
> Edgar Allan Poe

The David Foster Wallace Archive at the Harry Ransom
Center, University of Texas, contains more than 300 books
from the writer's library. Nearly all of them – including
those above – contain his annotations, underlinings,
doodles and occasional coffee cup rings. The result is a
very personal window into Wallace's thoughts and state
of mind as he read and worked. As well as many mentions
of family relationships, researcher Mike Miley has shown
that Wallace's initials (either DFW or DW) appear regularly next to passages about the act of creating or of failing
to create.

Wallace even marked up his American Heritage
Dictionary. These are the words circled:

abulia	invidious	quinate
benthos	jacal	rebus
cete	kohl	suint
distichous	legatee	talion
exergue	mendacious	uxorious
fraktur	neroli	valgus
gravid	ort	witenagemot
hypocorism	peccant	

Of course Wallace is not alone in writing in his books. Graham Greene wrote tens of thousands of comments in his personal library and there are half a dozen volumes of Samuel Taylor Coleridge's marginalia, which run from single words up to entire essays. In a copy of Henry David Thoreau's *A Week on the Concord and Merrimack Rivers*, which Jack Kerouac borrowed from a library in 1949, he underlined and ticked the phrase 'The traveler must be born again on the road'. Similarly, Kerouac added to his copy of Dostoyevsky's *An Unpleasant Predicament* – by the side of the word 'fond' he wrote 'fond always gives a batty tone, just right' and when he used the word 'actual' added 'Dusty's way of being a card'.

One of the most accessible collections of writers' additions is the online resource *Melville's Marginalia Online* at melvillesmarginalia.org. As well as a catalogue of all the books owned and borrowed by the author of *Moby-Dick*, it also shows all his markings and annotations in books such as Giorgio Vasari's *Lives of the Most Eminent Painters* and Thomas Warton's *History of English Poetry*.

The habit is not just limited to professional writers. Singer, actor, icon and King, Elvis Presley was also a keen reader who was particularly interested in philosophy, spirituality and the occult. He not only read books, but he also had no qualms about underlining passages and annotating them, not just on the pages but also sometimes on the covers. In one of his books about Mahatma Koot Hoomi, one of the Mahatmas that inspired the founding of the Theosophical Society, Elvis wrote: 'God loves you, but He loves you best when you sing'. His personal copy of *The Prophet* by Kahlil Gibran, a book he frequently gave to friends as he liked it so much, has numerous notes written by Elvis, including on page 22, 'There is always room to be more of a giver'.

BJARGVÆTTURINN Í GRASINU: THE CATCHER IN THE RYE IN TRANSLATION

Der Fänger im Roggen (German)
Hver tar sin – så får vi andre ingen (Norwegian)
Çavdar Tarlasında Çocuklar (Turkish)
El guardián entre el centeno (Spanish)
L'attrape-coeurs (French)
De vanger in het graan (Dutch)
Il giovane Holden (Italian)
O Apanhador no Campo de Centeio (Portuguese)
Rai Mugi Batake de Tsukamaete (Japanese)
Zabhegyezō (Hungarian)
Nad propastju vo rzhi (Russian)
Forbandede Ungdom (Danish)
Raddaren i noden (Swedish)
Buszujacy w Zbuzu (Polish)
Mai tian bu shou (Chinese)
Bjargvætturinn í grasinu (Icelandic)
Sieppari Ruispellossa (Finnish)

It's hard to name a language into which the Harry Potter books have not been translated. Faroese? Tick. Kalaallisut, a dialect in Greenland? Tick. Basque, Catalan and Galician? Tick, tick, tick. Classics teacher Andrew Wilson has even translated it into Ancient Greek, taking the style of Lucian as his inspiration. 'My intention,' he says, 'was to recreate a version of the book which would make sense to a Greek from any era up to the 4th century A.D.'

Translating books is a complex task. Simply coming up with an alternate title is a challenge, taking into account linguistic and cultural issues so that nothing is lost in translation. *Harry Potter and the Philosopher's Stone* often features an additional 'wizard' or 'sorcerer' in translation, while the Goblet of Fire occasionally morphs into a bowl, cup or chalice.

This list is a selection of ways in which translators have chosen to render *The Catcher in the Rye* by J.D. Salinger. Some of these, such as the German, Japanese (Haruki Murakami has translated it, as well as *The Great Gatsby*, *The Long Goodbye* and *Breakfast at Tiffany's*) and Turkish, are either exact translations or very similar (rye sometimes becomes corn or grain). Others take a less literal approach so that in Norwegian the book becomes 'Each Take One and the Others Get None', in Hungarian 'A Sharpener of Oats', and in Danish 'Damned Youth'. Some languages have had several different attempts. One of the Spanish variations was *El cazador oculto* ('The Hidden Hunter').

Of course it works the other way too. So while *The Great Gatsby* is *En Man Utan Skrupler* in Swedish or 'A Man Without Scruples', Stieg Larsson's *The Girl with the Dragon Tattoo* was actually *Män som hatar kvinnor* in the original, or 'Men Who Hate Women', and *The Girl Who Kicked the Hornets' Nest* was *Luftslottet som sprängdes*, 'The Air Castle that was Blown Up'. Meanwhile, German bestseller *Krabat* by Otfried Preussler became *The Satanic Mill* and *The Curse of the Darkling Mill* in English.

And it's not just the titles; the names of the characters also mutate. Jennings, the eponymous hero of Anthony Buckeridge's light-hearted schoolboy stories, is known as Bennett in France, Johnny in Brazil, Fredy in Germany and Stompa in Norway. Indeed, the Norwegian versions were rewritten rather than simply translated to give it a stronger Norwegian flavour. Not so happily, J.R.R. Tolkien was very upset when Bilbo Baggins became Bimbo Backlin in the Swedish translation of *The Lord of the Rings* and immediately put together a 23-page guide to the names in the books to help future translators.

BOOKS 'WRITTEN' BY SHERLOCK HOLMES

Practical Handbook of Bee Culture, with Some Observations upon the Segregation of the Queen
Upon the Distinction Between the Ashes of the Various Tobaccos
Upon the Tracing of Footsteps
The Influence of a Trade upon the Form of the Hand
On the Dating of Manuscripts
Upon the Polyphonic Motets of Lassus
Secret Writings
A Study of the Chaldean Roots in the Ancient Cornish Language
Upon Tattoo Marks
On the Variability of Human Ears (two monographs)

Some books are not merely difficult to track down, they are literally impossible to find. Because they don't exist. One of the earliest descriptions of these 'invisible books' is by Thomas Browne in his late 18th-century *Musaeum Clausum*, a fake catalogue of items including Aristotle's *de Precationibus*, Pytheas's account of travels beyond Ultima Thule, and a history of Hannibal's expedition through the Alps which is better than Livy's. Around fifty years later, Charles Lamb describes such things as 'biblia a-biblia' in his essay 'Detached Thoughts on Books and Reading'. Arguably the most popular modern non-book is *The Hitchhiker's Guide to the Galaxy* published by Megadodo Publications.

So while Sherlock Holmes is known to have 'written' 'The Blanched Soldier 'and 'The Lion's Mane', which were both published in the *Strand* magazine, he also had enough time on his hands to produce the list above (some of which, the great man reveals, were translated into French by his fellow detective François le Villard). *The Influence of a Trade upon the Form of the Hand* sounds particularly intriguing as it contains 'lithotypes of the hands of slaters, sailors, cork-cutters, compositors, weavers and diamond-polishers'.

In addition he mentions at various points that he is planning to write monographs on malingering, the typewriter's relation to crime, and the use of dogs in the work of the detective, not to mention a hugely ambitious textbook about the whole art of detection. Moriarty, in comparison, only managed to produce *The Dynamics of an Asteroid*.

Invented books feature heavily throughout Anthony Powell's twelve-volume *A Dance to the Music of Time*, not least the narrator Nick Jenkins's book about Robert Burton, *Borage and Hellebore*. Regularly mentioned throughout the series is *Fields of Amaranth* by St John Clarke, the title taken from Walter Savage Landor's *Aesop and Rhodopè*:

> There are no fields of amaranth on this side of the grave:
> there are no voices, O Rhodopè, that are not soon mute, however
> tuneful:
> there is no name, with whatever emphasis of passionate love repeated,
> of which the echo is not faint at last.

Other titles include *Camel Ride to the Tomb* by F.X. Trapnel (a character based on novelist Julian Maclaren-Ross), whose biography — *Death's Head Swordsman, The Life and Works of X. Trapnel* — is then 'written' by Russell Gwinnett. There is also *I Stopped at a Chemist* by Ada Leintwardine, which is then turned into the successful film, *Sally Goes Shopping*. Elsewhere, François Rabelais's novel series *Gargantua and Pantagruel* is littered with bizarrely titled imaginary books such as *Astrology's Chimney Sweep*, *Bell Ringers' Ballgames*, *Commercial Rope Tricks* and *Peas in Lard* (and many with more scabrous titles).

A variation on the theme appears in 'The Library of Dream' in Neil Gaiman's *The Sandman*. This contains books by, mostly, real authors, but the titles are variations on their best-known works and only exist in the writers' own dreams. Here is a selection from the shelves:

Road Trips to the Emerald City by L. Frank Baum
Tarzan in Mars by Edgar Rice Burroughs
Alice's Journey Behind the Moon by Lewis Carroll
Love Can Be Murder by Raymond Chandler
The Man Who Was October by G.K. Chesterton
The Return of Edwin Drood by Charles Dickens
The Conscience of Sherlock Holmes by Arthur Conan Doyle
Rooms by Neil Gaiman

The Merrie Comedie of the Redemption of Dr Faustus by
 Christopher Marlowe
The Ring and the Phoenix by E. Nesbit
The Fall of Gormenghast by Mervyn Peake
Arthur in Avalon by T.H. White
Psmith and Jeeves by P.G. Wodehouse

This is probably a homage to a similar kind of library of books planned but never written, which is mentioned in James Branch Cabell's 1919 *Beyond Life* and which includes *The Complete Works of David Copperfield*.

Then there are slightly mind-blowing Russian-doll-like books within books within books, such as *The Blind Assassin* by Margaret Atwood (the multiple story depths include part of *The Blind Assassin* by Laura Chase), and Italo Calvino's *If on a Winter's Night a Traveller* which is a tail-chasing labyrinth of titles.

And finally, in a case of life imitating art imitating life, some non-books have now actually been published. J.K. Rowling's *Harry Potter* series features dozens of imaginary titles, including three fictional ones which you can now read, *Quidditch Through the Ages* by Kennilworthy Whisp, *Fantastic Beasts and Where to Find Them* by Newt Scamander, and *The Tales of Beedle the Bard*. Other examples of phantom books now mysteriously appearing in print include Holmes's works on ash and bees, as well as H.P. Lovecraft's textbook of magic, *Necronomicon*.

WINNERS OF THE BOOKSELLER/
DIAGRAM PRIZE

American Bottom Archaeology by Charles Bareis and
    James Porter
If You Want Closure in Your Relationship, Start with Your Legs
    by Big Boom
Lesbian Sadomasochism Safety Manual by Pat Califia
The Joy of Sex: Pocket Edition by Alex Comfort
Living with Crazy Buttocks by Kaz Cooke
Reusing Old Graves: A Report on Popular British Attitudes by
    Douglas Davies and Alastair Shaw
Versailles: The View from Sweden by Elaine Dee and
    Guy Walton
Cooking with Poo by Saiyuud Diwong
Oral Sadism and the Vegetarian Personality by Glenn
    Ellenbogen
Butterworths Corporate Manslaughter Service by Gerard Forlin
*The Madam as Entrepreneur: Career Management in House
    Prostitution* by Barbara Sherman Heyl
*People Who Don't Know They're Dead: How They Attach
    Themselves to Unsuspecting Bystanders and What to Do
    About It* by Gary Leon Hill
How to Poo on a Date by Mats & Enzo
*How to Shit in the Woods: An Environmentally Sound Approach
    to a Lost Art* by Kathleen Meyer
*The Stray Shopping Carts of Eastern North America: A Guide to
    Field Identification* by Julian Montague
The Joy of Chickens by Dennis Nolan
*The 2009–2014 World Outlook for 60-Milligram Containers
    of Fromage Frais* by Philip M. Parker

Goblinproofing One's Chicken Coop by Bakeley Reginal

Bombproof Your Horse by Rick Pelicano and Lauren Tjaden

Strangers Have the Best Candy by Margaret Meps Schulte

Too Naked For the Nazis by Alan Stafford

Highlights in the History of Concrete by C.C. Stanley

Weeds in a Changing World: British Crop Protection Council Symposium Proceedings No. 64 by Charles H. Stirton

The Big Book of Lesbian Horse Stories by Alisa Surkis and Monica Nolan

Crocheting Adventures with Hyperbolic Planes by Daina Taimina

How to Avoid Huge Ships by John W. Trimmer

Unsolved Problems of Modern Theory of Lengthwise Rolling by A.I. Tselikov, G.S. Nikitin and S.E. Rokotyan

Greek Rural Postmen and Their Cancellation Numbers by Derek Willan

Developments in Dairy Cow Breeding: New Opportunities to Widen the Use of Straw by Gareth Williams

The Book of Marmalade: Its Antecedents, Its History, and Its Role in the World Today by Anne Wilson

Natural Bust Enlargement with Total Power: How to Increase the Other 90% of Your Mind to Increase the Size of Your Breasts by Donald Wilson

Managing a Dental Practice: The Genghis Khan Way by Michael R. Young

Designing High Performance Stiffened Structures by IMechE (Institution of Mechanical Engineers) (various authors)

Last Chance at Love: Terminal Romances (various authors)

Population and Other Problems: Family Planning, Housing 1,000 Million, Labour Employment (various authors)

Proceedings of the Second International Workshop on Nude Mice (various authors)

There are book prizes and then there are book prizes. Judges of the annual Bulwer-Lytton Fiction Contest require that entrants 'compose the opening sentence to the worst of all possible novels' while the *Literary Review* magazine's Bad Sex in Fiction Award has been going strong since Melvyn Bragg was the inaugural winner in 1993 for *A Time to Dance* (other winners have included Morrissey and Norman Mailer as well as John Updike, who won a Lifetime Achievement Award in 2008).

Even the most prolific of readers, though, will not have many of the above titles on their bookshelves, as these are the winners of the Bookseller/Diagram Prize for Oddest Title of the Year. Early champions were decided by a judging panel, but since the turn of the millennium it has been entirely down to a public vote. Self-published works are also now able to compete and indeed the 2014 prize went to the self-published *Strangers Have the Best Candy*. Although there is no monetary award for the winning author, the person who nominates the winning entry receives a 'passable bottle of claret'.

Not all the titles are quite what they appear, this being an 'odd title' competition rather than an 'odd book' one. While *How to Poo on a Date* does indeed do what it says on the tin, *Cooking with Poo* is simply a Thai cookbook by an author whose nickname is 'Poo'. Similarly, the full title of *Bombproof Your Horse* is *Teach Your Horse to Be Confident, Obedient, and Safe, No Matter What You Encounter*. Sometimes the method of writing the book is also a bit unusual. The 2009–2014 *World Outlook for 60-Milligram Containers of Fromage Frais* was computer-generated.

There have also been two special 'Diagram of Diagrams'

to mark the 15th and the 30th anniversaries of the prize. Proceedings of the Second International Workshop on Nude Mice won in 1993 and Greek Rural Postmen and Their Cancellation Numbers in 2008.

BOOKS THAT HAVE NEVER BEEN WRITTEN

The Man with the Shredded Ear

All Guns Are Loaded

Choice of Dessert

Return from Ruin

Here It Is Saturday

My Best to the Bride

The Man Who Loved the Rain

The Corpse Came in Person

Law Is Where You Buy It

The Porter Rose at Dawn

We All Liked Al

Fair With Some Rain

They Only Murdered Him Once

Too Late for Smiling

The Diary of a Loud Check Suit

Deceased When Last Seen

Quick, Hide the Body

A Night in the Ice Box

Goodnight and Goodbye

The Cool-Off

Uncle Watson Wants to Think

The Parson in the Parlour

Stop Screaming – It's Me

No Third Act

Twenty Minutes' Sleep

They Still Come Honest

Between Two Liars

The Lady with the Truck

The Black-Eyed Blonde

Rigadoo

Thunder Bug

Everyone Says Good-bye Too Soon

In 1985, shortly before he died, Italo Calvino told his wife Esther that he intended to write at least a dozen more books. While some of his work was gathered posthumously in The Road to San Giovanni, there are some which exist only in title form, including 'Instructions for the Other Self', 'Cuba' and 'The Objects'.

Other writers have far lengthier lists in their notebooks of good ideas for titles that never got written. The list at the top is Raymond Chandler's. He also invented a writer, Aaron Klopstein. Before killing himself with an Amazonian blow gun, Klopstein 'wrote' two novels called *Once More the Cicatrice* and *The Seagull Has No Friends*, two volumes of poetry (*The Hydraulic Facelift* and *Cat Hairs in the Custard*), one book of short stories (*Twenty Inches of Monkey*) and a book of critical essays, *Shakespeare in Baby Talk*.

Meanwhile, here is what F. Scott Fitzgerald mulled over:

Journal of a Pointless Life	*Thumbs Up*
Wore Out His Welcome	*The Bed in the Ball Room*
Your Cake	Book of burlesque entitled
Jack a Dull Boy	*These My Betters*
Dark Circles	Title for bad novel: *God's*
The Parvenu Hat	*Convict*
Talks to a Drunk	*Skin of His Teeth*
Tall Women	*Picture-Minded*
Birds in the Bush	*Love of a Lifetime*
Travels of a Nation	*Gwen Barclay in the Twentieth*
Don't You Love It?	*Century*
All Five Senses	*Result – Happiness*
Napoleon's Coat	*Murder of My Aunt*
Tavern Music, Boat Trains	*Police at the Funeral*
Dated	*The District Eternity*

Philosopher and critic George Steiner has even written a book – *My Unwritten Books* – about the seven books he has never managed to write, which would cover:

Chinese culture and Joseph Needham, expert in Chinese
    science
13th-century Italian writer Cecco d'Ascoli (who himself
    left many works unpublished) and the concept of literary
    competition and envy
Jewish identity
A survey of formal education techniques in various countries
What separates humans from animals
The concept of privacy
An erotic memoir with a focus on sexual linguistics

One of the most prolific non-finishers was Samuel Taylor Coleridge, who loved making lists of possible books/ poems to write and then not doing so. 'You spawn plans like a herring', Robert Southey told him, and Coleridge himself admitted that 'I lay too many Eggs in the hot Sands of this Wilderness, the World!' His notebooks are stuffed full of ideas lists, including this one:

An Essay on Tobit
On the art of prolonging Life – by getting up in a morning
On Marriage – in opposition to French Principles
Ode to a Looking Glass
Burnet's de montibus in English Blank Verse
Escapes from Misery – a Poem – Halo round the candle –
    Sigh visible
Life of David – a Sermon
Wild Poem on Maniac
Ode on St Withold

Crotchets

Hymns to the Sun, the Moon, and the Elements – six hymns –
  in one of them to introduce a dissection of Atheism

Egomist, a metaphysical Rhapsody

Ode to Southey

Ode to a Moth – against accumulation

Berkley's Maxims

Adventures of Christian, the mutineer

Military anecdotes

Hymn to Dr Darwin – in the manner of the Orphics

History of Phrases

Satire addressed to a Young Man who intended to study
  medicine at Edinburgh

THE FAKE BOOKS OF CHARLES DICKENS

Five Minutes in China
Forty Winks at the Pyramids
Abernethy on the Constitution
A Carpenter's Bench of Bishops
Toot's Universal Letter-Writer
Orson's Art of Etiquette
Downeaster's Complete Calculator
History of the Middling Ages
Jonah's Account of the Whale
Captain Parry's Virtues of Cold Tar
Kant's Ancient Humbugs
Bowwowdom. A Poem
The Quarrelly Review
The Gunpowder Magazine

Steele. By the Author of 'Ion'
The Art of Cutting the Teeth
Matthew's Nursery Songs
Paxton's Bloomers
On the Use of Mercury by the Ancient Poets
Drowsy's Recollections of Nothing
Heavyside's Conversations with Nobody
Commonplace Book of the Oldest Inhabitant
Growler's Gruffiology, with Appendix
The Books of Moses and Sons
Burke (of Edinburgh) on the Sublime and Beautiful
Teazer's Commentaries
King Henry the Eighth's Evidences of Christianity
Miss Biffin on Deportment
Morrison's Pills Progress
Lady Godiva on the Horse
Munchausen's Modern Miracles
Richardson's Show of Dramatic Literature
*Hansard's Guide to Refreshing Sleep (as many volumes as
    possible)*
History of a Short Chancery Suit
Catalogue of Statues of the Duke of Wellington

One of the 19th-century fads among England's literati was to decorate rooms with ornamental books instead of actual bookcases, often using humorous titles. Thomas Hood put together a particularly extensive trompe l'oeil library at Chatsworth in 1831 (later embellished with titles by Patrick Leigh Fermor in the 1960s) and in 1851, and so did Charles Dickens when he moved into Tavistock House in London. Here is his letter to local bookbinder Thomas

Robert Eeles, in which he enclosed the above list of his own home-made titles:

> Household Words' Office,
> Wednesday Evening, Oct. 22nd, 1851
> Dear Mr. Eeles,
> I send you the list I have made for the book-backs. I should like the
> 'History of a Short Chancery Suit' to come at the bottom of one
> recess, and the 'Catalogue of Statues of the Duke of Wellington' at the
> bottom of the other. If you should want more titles, and will let me
> know how many, I will send them to you.

While many of the titles are clever wordplay, others refer to famous Victorians. Miss Biffin was a Victorian mouth painter with no arms and vestigial legs, James Morrison sold quack 'cure-all' pills, and Captain Parry was an Arctic explorer who also features in the Chatsworth 'library' ('Captain Parry, Designs for Friezes'). Dickens also specified the length of some titles, so Five Minutes in China comes in three volumes, as does Drowsy's Recollections of Nothing. He seems to have been very pleased with the results, which were displayed in his study.

> Tavistock House, Tavistock Square, Nov. 17th, 1851
> Dear Mr Eeles,
> I must thank you for the admirable manner in which you have done
> the book-backs in my room. I feel personally obliged to you, I assure
> you, for the interest you have taken in my whim, and the prompti-
> tude with which you have completely carried it out.

In fact he was so pleased that he repeated the design when he moved to Gad's Hill in Kent, and even added more titles. The books here form part of a remarkably well-disguised bookcase-door to his study. This is the second list:

Life and Letters of the Learned Pig
The Pleasures of Boredom. (A Poem.)
Was Shakespeare's Father Merry?
Was Shakepeare's Mother Fair?
General Tom Thumb's Modern Warfare
Woods and Forests. By Peter the Wild Boy
Treatise on the Tapeworm by Tim Bobbin
Malthus's Nursery Songs
Hudson's Complete Failure
Adam's Precedents
Cockatoo on Perch
Swallows on Emigration
Waterworks. (By Father Mathew.)
Shelley's Oysters
The Scotch Fiddle. (Burns)
Cats' Lives
Groundsel. (By the author of Chickweed)
Chickweed
Drouett's Farming
Mag's Diversions
The Cook's Oracle
The Delphin Oracle
Critts' Edition of Meller
Hoyle on the Turnip
Butcher's Suetonius
Noah's Arkitecture

The Locomotive Engine explained by Colonel Sibthorpe
Acoustics. (Cod Sounds)
Optics. (Hooks and Eyes)
Strut's Walk
Haydn's Commentaries
Richardson's Show of Dramatic Literature
Socrates on Wedlock
The Virtues of our Ancestors
The Wisdom of our Ancestors
Phrenology (Italian Organ)

Again, among the witticisms – *Cats' Lives* comes in nine volumes – are topical references. Colonel Sibthorpe was an MP known for the range of movements he opposed, from Catholic and Jewish emancipation and the Reform Act of 1832 to the Great Exhibition. He also believed rail travel would never take off and stagecoaches would make a comeback. *Mag's Diversions* was an early working title for *David Copperfield. Drouett's Farming* is a reference to the man of the same name who ran a ramshackle residential school for pauper children and about whom Dickens wrote several very critical articles.

Dickens's fakes enjoyed a reincarnation as part of the New York Public Library's exhibition *Charles Dickens: The Key to Character.* As part of the 200th anniversary of the writer's birth, curators recreated several titles from the bookcases for the show.

KANSAS CITY LIBRARY'S COMMUNITY BOOKSHELF

Kansas City Stories Volume 1
Kansas City Stories Volume 2
Catch-22 by Joseph Heller
Children's Stories
Silent Spring by Rachel Carson
O Pioneers! by Willa Cather
Cien Años de Soledad (One Hundred Years of Solitude) by
  Gabriel García Márquez
Their Eyes Were Watching God by Zora Neale Hurston
Fahrenheit 451 by Ray Bradbury
The Republic by Plato
The Adventures of Huckleberry Finn by Mark Twain
Tao Te Ching by Lao Tzu
The Collected Poems of Langston Hughes by Langston Hughes
Black Elk Speaks by Black Elk, as told to John G. Neihardt
Invisible Man by Ralph Ellison
To Kill a Mockingbird by Harper Lee
Journals of the Expedition by Meriwether Lewis and William
  Clark
*Undaunted Courage: Meriwether Lewis, Thomas Jefferson, and
  the Opening of the American West* by Stephen Ambrose
The Lord of the Rings by J.R.R. Tolkien
A Tale of Two Cities by Charles Dickens
Charlotte's Web by E.B. White
Romeo and Juliet by William Shakespeare
Truman by David G. McCullough

Kansas City's new Central Library is a marvellous book palace. Formerly the First National Bank, the building was transformed to include a cinema in the old bank's basement vault and an enchanting section for children. And among its impressive holdings is the Ramos Collection, which contains a wealth of materials relating to African American history and culture. So it seems slightly unfair that its worldwide fame rests on its car park.

Granted, it is no ordinary car park. Looking more like something from an amusement park, its exterior – which spans a whole block – is decorated with twenty-two gigantic book spines known as the Community Bookshelf, each one 25 feet tall and 9 feet across (the list above is the running order from west to east on 10th Street between Wyandotte Street and Baltimore Avenue, with the building's entrance between *Huck Finn* and *Tao Te Ching*). Together, they do a marvellous job of cloaking the car park's staircases and are bookended by two stairwells.

Although there are twenty-two spines, three of them contain numerous individual titles. So the full list is actually:

KANSAS CITY STORIES, VOLUME 1

Kansas City, Missouri; Its History and Its People 1808–1908 by Carrie Westlake Whitney

Tom's Town, Kansas City and the Pendergast Legend by William M. Reddig

Goin' to Kansas City by Nathan W. Pearson, Jr

Farm: A Year in the Life of an American Farmer by Richard Rhodes

Mr Anonymous, the Story of William Volker by Herbert C. Cornuelle

Kansas City, Missouri: An Architectural History, 1826–1990 by
    George Ehrlich
Journeys Through Time: A Young Traveler's Guide to Kansas City's
    History by Monroe Dodd and Daniel Serda

KANSAS CITY STORIES, VOLUME II
Virgil Thomson, a Reader: Selected Writings 1924–1984
Mrs Bridge by Evan S.Connell
I Was Right on Time by Buck O'Neil
The O'Donnells by Peggy Sullivan
Independence Avenue by Eileen Bluestone Sherman
Stella Louella's Runaway Book by Lisa Campbell Ernst
PrairyErth: (A Deep Map) by William Least Heat-Moon
Messages from my Father by Calvin Trillin

CHILDREN'S STORIES:
Goodnight Moon by Margaret Wise Brown, pictures by
    Clement Hurd
Harold and the Purple Crayon by Crockett Johnson
Winnie the Pooh by A.A. Milne
Green Eggs and Ham by Dr Seuss
What a Wonderful World by Bob Thiele, George David Weiss
    and Tim Hopgood
Little House on the Prairie by Laura Ingalls Wilder
The Wonderful Wizard of Oz by L. Frank Baum
M.C. Higgins, the Great by Virginia Hamilton

Put together by specialist company Dimensional Innovations,
the facade is signboard Mylar on an aluminium frame.
Photographs were taken of original rare books and then
slightly modified for use, while clear Plexiglas windows

in the spines allow light to illuminate the car park. Unsurprisingly, the project has won a handful of awards.

Not only is it an artistic achievement, it is also a civic success. The concept of 'placemaking' is focused on how public spaces can be rethought with input from the local popular and community groups. In this instance, local users of the library suggested both the bookshelf idea and which titles should be used for the project of prettifying the car park structure. These were then whittled down by the Kansas City Public Library Board of Trustees.

Among other urban fake spine collections is De Batavier in Amsterdam, where artist Sanja Medic's ceramic and brick construction features 250 spines of famous Dutch poets and writers.

LOST BOOKS

Collected Plays of Agathon
Aristotle's Poetics, Book II, on Comedy
Lord Byron's Memoirs
The Isle of the Cross by Herman Melville
Ur-Hamlet

In his *If on a Winter's Night a Traveller* (*Se una notte d'inverno un viaggiatore*), Italo Calvino puts together a list of types of books found in a bookshop. So as well as 'Books You Haven't Read' there are 'Books That Everybody's Read So It's As If You Had Read Them Too' and 'Books You Want to Own So They'll Be Handy Just in Case'. It's an exhaustive rundown, but one missing category is 'Books You Can't

Buy Because Sadly They Have Been Lost Forever'.

This list above scarcely scratches the surface of what we had and now have not. So, while Agathon was important enough to merit a mention in Plato's *Symposium*, none of his plays have survived. *The History of Cardenio* by William Shakespeare and John Fletcher was certainly staged in 1613, but unless something remarkable happens certainly won't be again.

Some works are merely incomplete. Happily, we have quite a lot of the poem 'The Battle of Maldon', written around the 10th century and the inspiration for J.R.R. Tolkien's own poem 'The Homecoming of Beorhtnoth Beorhthelm's Son'. Sadly, we do not have the beginning or the ending. Similarly, only two out of the ten plays from the Coventry Mystery Plays cycle have made it down to our time.

Sometimes not only do we not have the work, we are not even sure about the author. The *Inventio Fortunata* travelogue focusing on a journey to the North Atlantic, dating from around the 1360s, was probably written by a Franciscan friar, but that's frankly still a bit of a guess since it had disappeared by 1500. Was the lost play Ur-*Hamlet*, a fore-runner of *Hamlet*, written by dramatist Thomas Kyd or William Shakespeare?

There are all kinds of reasons for loss, including the wholesale destruction of libraries, such as Alexandria's famous collection, and the deliberate ravaging of the monastic shelves during the 16th-century Dissolution of the Monasteries in England.

One of the main causes of loss is burning. Only three personal letters between George and Martha Washington survive, because she burned the lot on his death in 1799.

Lord Byron's two volumes of memoirs ended in the flames in 1824 because his publishers and executors were keen to protect what remained of his reputation. Gerard Manley Hopkins threw all his early poetry into the fire. And since 1985 nobody has been able to read Philip Larkin's diaries, although their annotated covers are still with us.

Other works have simply disappeared. When cultural critic Walter Benjamin committed suicide in 1940, he had a suitcase with him which contained an unknown Benjamin manuscript. It has never been tracked down. Sylvia Plath's unfinished second novel *Double Exposure* is also nowhere to be found, although there is a theory that there are draft copies knocking around if you know where to look...

NOT THE GREAT GATSBY

Among Ash-Heaps and Millionaires
Trimalchio in West Egg
On the Road to West Egg
Under the Red, White and Blue
Gold-Hatted Gatsby
The High-Bouncing Lover

Choosing a title for your newly finished masterpiece can be a tricky process. F. Scott Fitzgerald came up with all the above ideas before finally settling on the famous one, largely because of his editor Max Perkins (although he still grumbled about it after it was published). And of course he was not alone. Ernest Hemingway toyed with *I Have*

Committed Fornication But That Was in Another Country, and Besides the Wench Is Dead before sensibly settling on A Farewell to Arms. He also considered:

Love In War

Sorrow For Pleasure

Late Wisdom

The Enchantment

If You Must Love

World Enough and Time

In Praise of His Mistress

Every Night and All

Of Wounds and Other Causes

The Retreat from Italy

As Others Are

Love is One Fervent Fire

Kindlit without Desire

A World to See

Patriots Progress

The Grand Tour

The Italian Journey

The World's Room

Disorder and Early Sorrow

An Italian Chronicle

The Time Exchanged

Death Once Dead

They Who Get Shot

The Italian Experience

Love in Italy

Love in War

The Sentimental Education

Education of the Flesh

The Carnal Education

The Sentimental Education of
    Frederick Henry

Thing That Has Been

Nights and Forever

In Another Country

Knowledge Increaseth Sorrow

The Peculiar Treasure

One Event Happeneth To
    Them All

One Thing For Them All

Nothing Better For A Man

Time of War

The World's Romm

One Thing is Certain

The Long Home

So what is the best way of choosing a title? You could try the always popular Something's Something approach – Midnight's Children, Schindler's List, Homer's Daughter; equations such as author Andy Martin's useful 'number + noun

+ 'of' + noun' (e.g. *Seven Pillars of Wisdom*); and various random title generators (some are very specific, such as the online Malcolm Gladwell Book Generator which includes 'The Cheers Effect: How and Why Everybody Knows Your Name). Lulu.com even offers an automated way of checking if your title is likely to be a bestseller, generally suggesting that books with slightly more abstract titles, such as Agatha Christie's *Sleeping Murder*, have the greatest chances of success.

Another way is simply to borrow the best bits of other people's work, which is not only the way that Aldous Huxley usually went but can be turned into a Christmas quiz for the well read. So where do these Huxley titles come from originally? (answers opposite):

After Many a Summer Dies The Swan
Antic Hay
Beyond the Mexique Bay
The Doors of Perception
Eyeless in Gaza
Jesting Pilate
Those Barren Leaves

One problem with this method of choosing a title is that it requires you to be very well read (as Clive James has observed: 'Nowadays, the titles of his books are more alive than his books'). This is exactly what Huxley was. He had read everything and for good measure even travelled with a half-sized edition of the *Encyclopaedia Britannica* to make sure he had something decent to read.

As good luck would have it, there's a much easier way.

Just open your *Collected Works of Shakespeare* and off you go, an approach which also bore fruit for Huxley, who certainly perused his copies of *The Tempest* (*Brave New World*), *Macbeth* (*Brief Candles*), *Hamlet* (*Mortal Coils*), and *Henry IV Part 1* (*Time Must Have A Stop* – a bit of a cheat, this one, as the actual quote from Hotspur's death speech is 'But thought's the slave of life, and life time's fool; And time, that takes survey of all the world, Must have a stop').

Answers:

Tithonus by Alfred, Lord Tennyson
Edward II by Christopher Marlowe
Bermudas by Andrew Marvell
The Marriage of Heaven and Hell by William Blake
Samson Agonistes by John Milton
Of Truth by Francis Bacon
The Tables Turned by William Wordsworth

THE FIRST AUDIOBOOKS (AND OTHER SENSORY FICTION)

Typhoon by Joseph Conrad
The Murder of Roger Ackroyd by Agatha Christie
The Gospel According to St John
The Story of San Michele by Axel Munthe
There's Death in the Churchyard by William Gore

We use all our senses when we read and now sensory fiction is starting to take off in a big, sometimes slightly smelly, way.

Talking books have a much longer history than most people imagine. While children of the 1960s and 1970s will have fond memories of Johnny Morris reading the *Thomas the Tank Engine* stories on vinyl, Matt Rubery – audiobook historian, Reader in Nineteenth-Century Literature at Queen Mary, University of London, and author of *The Untold Story of the Talking Book* – has uncovered the first five books recorded by the Royal National Institute of Blind People in 1935 (listed above). These are probably the oldest talking book recordings made in Britain. Despite the cruelties of shellac, he is also making excellent progress in tracking down the remaining surviving recordings of each one. You can hear the *Gospel According to St John*, read beautifully clearly by BBC announcer Stuart Hibberd, online at www.aeolian.org.uk/rnib.

Now, of course, they have become so much part of the mainstream that the Public Lending Right started making payments on audiobook titles borrowed in 2014/15. Here were the ten most borrowed in that period:

1. *Without a Trace* by Lesley Pearse, read by Emma Powell
2. *Harry Potter and the Philosopher's Stone* by J.K. Rowling, read by Stephen Fry
3. *Harry Potter and the Deathly Hallows* by J.K. Rowling, read by Stephen Fry
4. *Demon Dentist* by David Walliams, read by David Walliams
5. *The Cuckoo's Calling* by Robert Galbraith, read by Robert Glenister
6. *Demon Dentist* by David Walliams, read by David Walliams [a separate edition from number 4]
7. *The Silkworm* by Robert Galbraith, read by Robert Glenister

8. *Never Go Back* by Lee Child, read by Jeff Harding
9. *Be Careful What You Wish For* by Jeffrey Archer, read by
   Alex Jennings
10. *Ratburger* by David Walliams, read by David Walliams

The Massachusetts Institute of Technology has taken the idea of sensory fiction several stages further and offers a Science Fiction to Science Fabrication course. Using a range of sensors and tools, part of the studies include building a wearable connected book contraption in the form of a strap-on vest. This allows the reader to get fully in contact with the character's emotions and physical states for a genuinely immersive reading experience. Selected passages trigger vibrations to influence heart rate, and the temperature of the vest can be similarly adjusted (for example making it warmer if you are reading about a sunny day). A compression element uses pressurised airbags to provide levels of constriction, and even the cover contains 150 LEDs which change appearance depending on what's happening on the page. The first story to be used with the book vest was, appropriately, *The Girl Who Was Plugged In* by James Tiptree Jr, the pen name of writer Alice Sheldon.

The course reading list features plenty of short stories, including those by Ursula K. Le Guin, Stanislaw Lem and Elizabeth Bear as well as these novels:

Neuromancer by William Gibson
Kill Decision by Daniel Suarez
Diamond Age by Neal Stephenson
Do Androids Dream of Electric Sheep? by Philip K. Dick
Riders of the Purple Wage by Philip Jose Farmer

For a gentler, more nose-centric experience, the discerning booklover is also now able to buy fragrances to augment their reading sessions. But this is no clunky 'scratch 'n sniff' solution. Paperback cologne spray from Demeter claims to be 'sweet and lovely with just a touch of the musty smell of aged paper ... it harnesses that scent with a sprinkling of violets and a dash of tasteful potpourri'. It claims to smell just like your favourite second-hand bookshop. Or maybe try Paper Passion Perfume, which says it 'captures the unique bouquet of freshly printed books'. A collaboration between perfumer Geza Schoen, publisher Gerhard Steidl and *Wallpaper* magazine, it 'expresses that peculiar mix of paper and ink which gives a book its unmistakable aroma, along with the fresh scent which a book opened for the first time releases'.

Or maybe invest in a candle. Paddywax's Library Candle series does not drill down to individual book titles but does supply you with around half a dozen writers including Edgar Allan Poe, Jane Austen, Charles Dickens, Mark Twain, Ralph Waldo Emerson and John Steinbeck. The Leo Tolstoy is its signature soy wax offering, featuring black plum, persimmon and oakmoss fragrance notes. Similarly, Frostbeard Studio's selection includes 'Gatsby's Mansion', 'Cliffs of Insanity' and 'Don't Panic (Fresh Towel)'. Its 'Shire' candle – oakmoss, clover, aloe and a hint of pipe tobacco – is the 'One candle you need by your side when embarking on an epic adventure'.

And if all other senses fail, for your taste buds, there's cake in the form of the annual International Edible Book Festival. With events around the world taking place on 1 April each year (but it's not an April Fool's joke, honest), there's bound to be something delicious near you, such as a Life of Pi.

THE UK'S TOP TWENTY REVISITED READS

1. The *Harry Potter* series by J.K. Rowling
2. *The Lord of the Rings* by J.R.R. Tolkien
3. *Pride and Prejudice* by Jane Austen
4. *The Hobbit* by J.R.R. Tolkien
5. *Jane Eyre* by Charlotte Bronte
6. *1984* by George Orwell
7. *The Da Vinci Code* by Dan Brown
8. *The Lion, The Witch and The Wardrobe* by C.S. Lewis
9. *Wuthering Heights* by Emily Bronte
10. *Catch-22* by Joseph Heller
11. *Notes from a Small Island* by Bill Bryson
12. *To Kill a Mockingbird* by Harper Lee
13. *Flowers in the Attic* by Virginia Andrews
14. *Black Beauty* by Anna Sewell
15. *Good Omens* by Neil Gaiman and Terry Pratchett
16. The Bible
17. *The Hitchhiker's Guide to the Galaxy* by Douglas Adams
18. *Bridget Jones's Diary* by Helen Fielding
19. *Gone with the Wind* by Margaret Mitchell
20. *Great Expectations* by Charles Dickens

Just over three-quarters of readers in the UK enjoy re-reading favourite books, according to a survey by Costa. Indeed, the 2007 poll – which resulted in this top twenty list – indicated that a sixth of us return to a much-loved book more than five times.

Costa's research also revealed that a third of people say they find something new each time they re-read, and 8 per cent do so because it's better than anything else they have read. A fifth do so because they find it comforting. In an article for the *Guardian* newspaper in 2012, writer Philip Hensher admitted he has read some of his favourite novels (such as P.G. Wodehouse's *The Code of the Woosters* and Laura Ingalls Wilder's *Little House in the Big Woods*) around thirty times. In the same article, Ian Rankin named his favourite re-reads as:

Rivals by Jilly Cooper
Bleak House by Charles Dickens
Four Quartets by T.S. Eliot
A Dance to the Music of Time by Anthony Powell
The Prime of Miss Jean Brodie by Muriel Spark

Looking at book selection from the opposite point of view, another survey for BBC Store in 2016 detailed the top twenty books people lied most about reading (coincidentally featuring several titles from the previous list):

Alice's Adventures in Wonderland by Lewis Carroll
1984 by George Orwell
The Lord of the Rings trilogy by J.R.R. Tolkien
War And Peace by Leo Tolstoy
Anna Karenina by Leo Tolstoy
The Adventures of Sherlock Holmes by Arthur Conan Doyle
To Kill A Mockingbird by Harper Lee
David Copperfield by Charles Dickens

Crime and Punishment by Fyodor Dostoyevsky
Pride and Prejudice by Jane Austen
Bleak House by Charles Dickens
Harry Potter series by J.K. Rowling
Great Expectations by Charles Dickens
The Diary of Anne Frank
Oliver Twist by Charles Dickens
Fifty Shades trilogy by E.L. James
And Then There Were None by Agatha Christie
The Great Gatsby by F. Scott Fitzgerald
Catch-22 by Joseph Heller
The Catcher in the Rye by J.D. Salinger

Overall, one in four said that they fibbed about reading classic novels when they were adapted successfully for television. As well as wanting to be part of the chat surrounding the programme, nearly two-thirds said they did so because they felt being well read made them more appealing, although more than 40 per cent said they would have a go at a classic if the major networks had deemed it important enough to film. In broad terms, Costa's survey showed that 43 per cent of people will finish a book if they make it past the first chapter. In the same way as people often make a snap judgement when making house-hunting viewings, around 4 per cent said they knew they would finish the book after reading just the first page.

Anybody particularly interested in this subject should re-read On Rereading by Patricia Meyer Spacks, Nothing Remains the Same by Wendy Lesser (which is also something of a bibliomemoir) and Rereadings: Seventeen Writers Revisit Books They Love by Anne Fadiman.

BOOKS OWNED BY RICHARD III

Beatae Katherinae Egyptiae Christi Sponsae Vita by Pietro
   Carmeliano
Historia Destructionis Troiae by Guido Delle Colonne
Chronicles of St Denis (in French)
The Fitzhugh Chronicle
Historia Regum Britanniae by Geoffrey of Monmouth
De Regimine Principum by Giles of Rome
Order of Chivalry by Ramon Lull (translated by William Caxton)
Siege of Thebes by John Lydate
The Booke of Gostlye Grace of Mechtild of Hackeborn
   (English translation)
De Re Militari by Publius Flavius Vegetius Renatus
Boke of Noblesse by William Worcester
Tristan & Isolde
A Book of Hours and Prayers
The Prophecy of the Eagle, and its Commentary
The Old and New Testament (English translation by John
   Wycliffe)
A collection of stories by Geoffrey Chaucer ('The Knight's Tale',
   'Clerk's Tale', 'Palamon and Arcite' and 'Griselda'), John Lydgate
   ('Siege of Troy') and Hugh de Rotelande ('Ipomedon')

Trying to reconstruct personal libraries 500 years after
their famous owner died is never an easy task, even when
that person was a monarch. Luckily, one thing makes it
easier when it comes to Richard III. He liked to write his
name in his books (either as Ricardus Rex or R Gloucestre).
Fine work has been done researching Richard's personal
library by Anne F. Sutton and Livia Visser-Fuchs, and their

various publications show that the king's collection reflects the fashionable reading of his day, a mixture of romance/chivalry, 'how to' government self-help books, history – the *Fitzhugh Chronicle* is a history of England from the 6th to the end of the 12th century – and religion. Among titles not so well known today are:

De Re Militari: an art-of-war manual from the late 4th century about Roman warfare, strategy and tactics, it was arguably the most influential military guide in the west up to the 19th century and probably influenced Machiavelli's *The Prince*. It contains the phrase normally translated as 'If you want peace, prepare for war' (*si vis pacem, para bellum*).

De Regimine Principum: inspired by the works of Aristotle, this 13th-century example of the 'mirrors for princes' genre contains advice to kings about how to behave virtuously, the importance of family life, and how to govern in peacetime and war.

Ipomedon: a 12th-century romance in which an undercover knight undertakes various quests, and battles three monsters before winning the hand of a princess.

Order of Chivalry: written originally in Catalan and one of the earliest books to be printed by William Caxton, Lull's eight chapters cover the history and theory of knighthood in a kind of rulebook style.

Not all royal books were quite so highbrow. Catherine Howard was given five books when she married Henry VIII, all of which were probably 'girdle books', decorative objects to be worn, dangling from a belt, rather than read for their intellectual content. They were:

Oone booke of golde ennamuled wherein is a clock. Upon
every syde if which booke is thre diamondes, a litle man
standing upon oone of them, foure turqueses and thre rubyes,
with a little cheyne of gold hanging on it as ennamuled.

Oone booke of gold ennamuled with blacke, garnesshed with
xxvii rubyes, having also a cheyne of golde and perle to
hange it by, conteignyng xliii peerlles.

Oone other booke ennamuled with grene, white and blewe,
havyng a feir sapher on euery side and viii rubyes upon the
same booke.

Oone other booke ennamuled with grene, white and red and
garnesshed with viii small rubyes, having H.I. ennamuled with
blacke, the backs of the same booke being glasse.

Oone booke of golde conteignyng xii diamondes and xl rubyes.

Girdle books, a kind of early iPad Mini, were also used
at Mass and for daily readings. None of Catherine's have
survived, and though girdle books are frequently depicted
in art, there are only about two dozen in existence today.

BIBLIOTHERAPY: BOOKS ON PRESCRIPTION

Kite Spirit by Sita Brahmachari
House of Windows by Alexia Casale
Mind Your Head by Juno Dawson, Dr Olivia Hewitt, Gemma
Correll
Quiet the Mind by Matthew Johnstone
Every Day by David Levithan
Blame My Brain: The Amazing Teenage Brain Revealed by
Nicola Morgan

I'll Give You the Sun by Jandy Nelson
*Stuff That Sucks: Accepting What You Can't Change and
    Committing to What You Can* by Ben Sedley
The Self-Esteem Team's Guide to Sex, Drugs and WTFs!? by
    The Self-Esteem Team (foreword by Zoella)

The theory that reading can help treat illness goes back to the ancient Greeks and Egyptians. Today in the UK, one in ten young people has a diagnosable mental health disorder and The Reading Agency has put together a range of book lists to support them as part of its 'Reading Well: Books on Prescription' scheme.

The titles above are for general use for those aged thirteen to eighteen, but the full list of thirty-five titles covers other categories including ADHD, anxiety, autism and Asperger syndrome, body image/eating disorders, bullying, confidence/self-esteem, depression, OCD, self-harm, stress and mood swings. All titles have been selected by experts in their field. As well as self-helps, memoirs and graphic novels, there is also a range of fiction including *The Curious Incident of the Dog in the Night-Time* by Mark Haddon and *The Perks of Being a Wallflower* by Stephen Chbosky.

Though an ancient concept, the term 'bibliotherapy' was invented by Samuel Crothers in 1916 in his article 'The Literary Clinic' for the magazine *Atlantic Monthly*. Over the last 100 years it has become an officially recognised and popular treatment, especially in the USA, using an ongoing process of identification, catharsis and insight. Evidence from the National Institute of Clinical Excellence (NICE) indicates that self-help reading can help people with common mental health conditions, such as anxiety and depression.

Reading Well: Books on Prescription provides reading lists for adults with common mental health conditions, people with dementia and their carers, and people with long-term conditions and their carers, as well as young people. Books can be recommended by GPs or other health professionals and of course anybody can also choose a book from their local library without a professional recommendation. The programme reached 635,000 people in its first three years.

Although some people may regard bibliotherapy as a slightly quacky form of medicine, the scheme is endorsed by NHS England and appears to work best when used alongside conventional therapies rather than replacing them. Ted Hughes said he wrote *The Iron Man* 'as a blueprint imaginative strategy for dealing with a neurosis ... It is a story intended to cure the mentally sick'. He added that he felt it was successful though hard to measure exactly.

Slightly less scientific, though still with many admirers, is the bibliotherapy service offered by The School of Life in London by Ella Berthoud and Susan Elderkin. They use fiction (and occasionally philosophy and poetry) to cope with daily life issues. Their recently published book *The Novel Cure: An A–Z of Literary Remedies* thus offers selections to deal with anything from addiction to coffee to zestlessness, including *Robinson Crusoe* as a cure for pessimism, and *White Noise* by Don DeLillo for those afflicted with a fear of death.

· BOOK LIST ART

A Day at the Beach by Robert Grenier
The Bathers by Lorenzo Thomas
Shark 1
Shark 2
Shark 3
Sudden Violence by Gregg Jones
Silence by John Cage

Book art has become a major industry, from turning classic covers into mugs to completely repurposing old/ unwanted/ruined books into new objects. Spines have attracted particular attention. Artist Simon Jones has reconfigured album tracks to look like the titles on classic Penguin and Pelican spines, so that you can now own poster prints of David Bowie's *Hunky Dory* or Bob Dylan's *Blood on the Tracks* looking like a casually put together pile of books. American artist Mike Stilkey has taken things a stage further and paints fantasy figures of people and animals directly on to the spines of book sculptures, some requiring thousands of books and reaching up to 24 feet high.

The list above is *A Day at the Beach*, an example from artist Nina Katchadourian's Sorted Project. By creatively aligning a chain of spines from various books and magazines, she produces poetry, aphorisms or very, very short stories which are then photographed for posterity.

Arrangement is important but plays a lesser part in Jane Mount's *Ideal Bookshelf* series for which she takes a theme, such as Coming of Age, then in gouache and ink paints a series of hand-lettered spines of appropriate books as if sitting on a bookshelf. So one of her two SciFi series is *Ideal Bookshelf 566* (books pictured left to right):

A Princess of Mars by Edgar Rice Burroughs
Snow Crash by Neal Stephenson
The Hitchhiker's Guide to the Galaxy by Douglas Adams
The Left Hand of Darkness by Ursula K. Le Guin
Ender's Game by Orson Scott Card
Ringworld by Larry Niven
A Canticle for Leibowitz by Walter M. Miller, Jr
Stranger in a Strange Land by Robert Heinlein
Do Androids Dream of Electric Sheep? by Philip K. Dick
A Journey to the Centre of the Earth by Jules Verne
Frankenstein by Mary Shelley
The Handmaid's Tale by Margaret Atwood
The Giver by Lois Lowry
Solaris by Stanislaw Lem
Childhood's End by Arthur C. Clarke

In 2012 she also published a book called *My Ideal Bookshelf* with writer Thessaly La Force, which featured her spine paintings of favourite books as chosen by 100 creative people including Patti Smith, Michael Chabon and fashion designers Kate and Laura Mulleavy of Rodarte.

When just a spine won't do, there is always the entire book to play with. An anonymous artist has been depositing a series of elaborate book sculptures at various locations around Scotland since 2011. An early theme was the work of Ian Rankin (specifically *Exit Music, Knots and Crosses, Hide and Seek, The Impossible Dead*). All the magnificent work was made from old books and came with labels supporting books and reading, and condemning cuts to library services.

In addition to her own work, the sculptor was also commissioned to create five book sculptures as part of Book Week Scotland in 2012. These were hidden in various locations and the finders' prizes were paper sculpture trophies of a teacup. The sculptures were inspired by:

Peter Pan by J.M. Barrie (this teacup had a spout with a hook-tip)
Tam O'Shanter by Robert Burns
Lanark: A Life in Four Books by Alasdair Gray
Whisky Galore by Compton Mackenzie
Treasure Island by Robert Louis Stevenson

BOOKS IKEA USES AS DECORATION IN ITS SHOPS

Café Musa by Tomas Andersson
Skramskott by Rolf Dahlstrom
En skörd av tårar by Edwidge Danticat
Min vän Mr Ho by Ulf Eriksson
Lille Erik från Lysebjär by Leif Evnell
Den amerikanska mardrömmen by Susan Faludi
Pytt i Panna by Guy Jamais
Barn i bildterapi by Barbro Luterkort
Den Vantade by Kathleen McGowan
Ett hus åt Mr Biswas by V.S. Naipaul
Att Ater Motas by Rosamunde Pilcher
Golden Gate by Vikram Seth

Fisk och kultur by Sjón
Främlingars dom by Andrew Taylor
Nedmontering by Anatolij Zlobin

Books not only furnish rooms, they also furnish shops. In his essay 'Books as Furniture', Nicholson Baker is inspired (by the unexpected use as a decorative prop of *The Wood-Carver of 'Lympus* by Mary E. Waller in The Company Store's catalogue) to analyse other clothing and furniture catalogues. His scrutiny of The Pottery Barn reveals that it appears to have a stock of around fifty titles for its shots. These include:

The Adventures of Augie March by Saul Bellow (hardback)
Tongues of Flame by Mary Ward Brown
Citizen of New Salem by Paul Horgan
A Rose for Virtue by Norah Lofts
A bound German periodical from 1877
A textbook of pathology from before the Second World War

IKEA – home to the multi-million-selling Billy bookcase – is perhaps the best-known example of books as popular dressing, with endless shelves of books seen throughout their international stores. The top list is a partial inventory of what is available in its Brent Park branch in London. There is no 'approved' list of books; titles are simply chosen as props depending on the individual situation, so that a 'room' designed for a student will have titles which IKEA believes would be popular with twentysomethings.

IKEA's selection inconspicuously blends into its surroundings, be that in an office situation or a mocked-up small apartment. The books perform a pleasantly decorative function, producing a welcoming atmosphere. Space is left on shelves for other bits and pieces to make it all feel more personal.

They are also something of an artistic statement. The spines of the books used are generally restrained, with only a dash of colour here and there. There is no organisation by blocks of bright colour or with the spines facing inward. Yet there is no pretence of this being a recreation of what your house might look like, so multiple copies of the same title are frequently shelved together.

Unless somebody has sneaked in something unsanctioned, every book is in Swedish. Some are translated, usually from authors writing in English such as Vikram Seth, Kathleen McGowan (*Den Vantade* is *The Expected One*) and Edwidge Danticat, the National Book Award-nominated Haiti-born writer who now lives in the USA. There is also the Icelandic author Sjón, whose *Fisk och kultur* became *The Whispering Muse* in English. But overwhelmingly these are Swedish fiction and non-fiction authors, though not those with which most shoppers will be familiar such as Henning Mankell or Stieg Larsson.

So Leif Evnell's *Lille Erik från Lysebjär* takes as its theme the movement from rural to urban areas in Sweden in the 1950s. It is told through the story of Lille Erik and her parents, who leave their farm and move to Monbijougatan in Malmo. Meanwhile, *Barn i bildterapi* by Barbro Luterkort looks at how art therapy works with children, focusing on ten case studies and how they develop over the course of the therapy. *Pytt i Panna* by Guy Jamais is a light-hearted miscellany of food and drink writing, and *Café Musa* by

Tomas Andersson is a travelogue through Egypt, from Alexandria and Cairo into the deserts and mountains, examining the country's long history as well as modern issues such as the role of Islam in its 21st-century life. It is the second part of a trilogy about Iran, Egypt and Turkey.

BIBLIOMEMOIRS: A LIST OF BOOK-LIST BOOKS

The Whole Five Feet: What the Great Books Taught Me About Life, Death and Pretty Much Everything Else by Christopher Beha

Great Books: My Adventures With Homer, Rousseau, Woolf, and Other Indestructible Writers of the Western World by David Denby

Out of Sheer Rage: Wrestling With D.H. Lawrence by Geoff Dyer

How to be a Heroine by Samantha Ellis

Ex Libris by Anne Fadiman

Outside of a Dog by Rick Gekoski

Tolkien's Gown by Rick Gekoski

Howards End Is on the Landing: A Year of Reading From Home by Susan Hill

Ten Years in the Tub: A Decade Soaking in Great Books by Nick Hornby

Why I Read: The Serious Pleasure of Books by Wendy Lesser

What W.H. Auden Can Do For You by Alexander McCall Smith

A Reading Diary: A Year of Favourite Books by Alberto Manguel

My Life in Middlemarch by Rebecca Mead

The Year of Reading Dangerously by Andy Miller

The Books in My Life by Henry Miller
Reading the World: Confessions of a Literary Explorer by
    Ann Morgan
Reading Lolita in Tehran: A Memoir in Books by Azar Nafisi
The Reading Promise: My Father and the Books We Shared by
    Alice Ozma
My Salinger Year by Joanne Rakoff
The Shelf: Adventures in Extreme Reading by Phyllis Rose
A Year of Reading Proust by Phyllis Rose
Tolstoy and the Purple Chair: My Year of Magical Reading by
    Nina Sankovitch
The End of Your Life Book Club by Will Schwalbe
The Child that Books Built by Francis Spufford

This last section is a list of books about lists of books. But
these are not the straightforward kind such as Melvyn
Bragg's 12 Books That Changed The World; these chart
personal relationships with specific titles and authors,
sometimes not entirely happy ones.

Rare-book dealer Rick Gekoski says he was the first to
coin the term 'bibliomemoir', using it in his book *Outside
of a Dog* which listed twenty-five books which have been
particularly special for him throughout his life, from
Horton Hatches the Egg by Dr Seuss via Roald Dahl's *Matilda*
to Ludwig Wittgenstein's *Philosophical Investigations*. Gekoski's
follow-up to *Outside of a Dog* was *Tolkien's Gown*, looking at
twenty modern classics and his involvement with first
editions of each one.

Arguably the Godfather of bibliomemoirists is Henry
Miller, whose *The Books in My Life* took a wide-ranging look
at how and what he read, covering issues such as reading

in the toilet and including a list of the 100 books that most influenced him, starting with the slightly vague 'Ancient Greek Dramatists' and ending up with Walt Whitman's 'Leaves of Grass'. It also features a section revealing which friends supplied him with books and another on those books he still intended to read (such as *The Pickwick Papers* by Charles Dickens). He promised a follow-up volume which he threatened would include everything he could remember reading. This never materialised.

Some bibliomemoirs simply recount a life in books. Anne Fadiman's *Ex Libris* looks at how to go about merging libraries when you get married, as well as recounting how she built dens out of her father's books as a child, while Samantha Ellis analyses how her heroines have influenced how she has lived her life. Although also focusing on the theme of heroism, Azar Nafisi's is a rather more serious memoir with sections entitled 'Lolita', 'Gatsby', 'James' and 'Austen', in which she examines the often oppressive challenges of life in Iraq in the 1980s and 1990s.

Others are accounts of specific projects. Christopher Beha read all fifty-one volumes of the Harvard Classics, a collection of books collectively measuring 5 feet, put together by Charles William Eliot, a former Harvard president. Eliot believed that together they provided 'a means of obtaining such a knowledge of ancient and modern literature as seems essential to the twentieth-century idea of a cultivated man'. (He upped the size from his original claim that 3 feet would be sufficient.) Andy Miller rounded up a similar number of books, what he describes as a 'List of Betterment', to tackle the classics that he – and, frankly, many others of us – have never read. The result is as much about a Croydon childhood and the Puffin Club as it is about *Beowulf* or Luke Rhinehart's *The Dice Man*. Phyllis Rose made a far more random choice when she decided to simply read everything on the LEQ to LES shelf in the New York Society Library.

Many bibliomemoirs tend to focus on a small range of titles – or even, like John Baxter's account of book-buying and dealing, *A Pound of Paper*, teeter on the edge of straight biography. Others, such as Rebecca Mead's, focus on a single author or work. At the other extreme is Susan Hill, who spent a year essentially re-reading her entire library rather than buying any new books (a year seems to be a key length of time for many bibliomemoirists, apart from Nick Hornby, who has written a decade of columns for *The Believer* magazine revealing what he has read and what he has bought month by month). At the end of the twelve months, she draws up a list of forty titles. While admitting that these are not the best ever written, they are the ones she thinks 'I could manage with alone, for the rest of my life'.